PERSUASIVE ADVOCACY

Cases for
Argumentation
and Debate

Halford Ross Ryan

Washington and Lee University

UNIVERSITY
PRESS OF
AMERICA

LANHAM • NEW YORK • LONDON

Library of Congress Cataloging in Publication Data

Ryan, Halford Ross.
  Persuasive advocacy.

  Bibliography: p.
  1. Debates and debating.   2. Forensic oratory.
I. Title.
PN4181.R93   1985   808.53   85-15030
ISBN 0-8191-4858-X (alk. paper)
ISBN 0-8191-4859-8 (pbk. : alk. paper)

ACKNOWLEDGMENTS

This book is a product of several salutary sources which are appropriately acknowledged here.

Dean John Elrod and President John Wilson, Washington and Lee University, provided the academic encouragement and the financial subvention, through The Glenn Grant Publication Fund, for this work. Their commitment to forensic scholarship at an undergraduate teaching institution is gratefully recorded.

Argumentation and debate students, in company with their intercollegiate debate counterparts, have practiced in the classroom and in countless intercollegiate debate tournament rounds some of the techniques and ideas for persuasive advocacy which are contained in these pages. Fortunately for a writer in forensics, debate is an academic activity in which the teacher may often times learn from those who would be taught. Their commitment to learn, and to teach, the skills of disputation by means of the moot legal cases contained herein are duly noted and appreciated.

Mention must be made of my forensic mentor, Professor Joseph O'Rourke, Wabash College. His lead in teaching debate as a speech course in the liberal arts curriculum and as a study of human communication is continued, hopefully, in this present volume.

One would naturally accept credit for the strengths of the moot murder cases in Section Two, but one must also accept the responsibility for their weaknesses. Yet one trusts that their advantages may outweigh their deficiencies.

Halford Ross Ryan
Lexington, Virginia

TABLE OF CONTENTS

INTRODUCTION

This slender volume is grounded in the belief that while many forensic students know how to debate well--and many very well--a number of debaters--and perhaps too many--do not know how to argue effectively. That is, many forensic speakers cannot argue persuasively. That belief has ensued from my fifteen years in the forensic classroom and in incalculable NDT-style intercollegiate debate rounds; from hosting, coaching, and observing numerous audience-style debates at colleges and universities in the United States and in Great Britain; and from the forensic literature which is either actually cited in the appropriate places or listed as additional readings.

The book is purposefully divided into two major sections. The first section treats of the history, terminology, and practice of persuasive advocacy in a debating situation. The debate student should have a firm foundation in the theory of debate before an informed practice of it can be accomplished. This important theoretical knowledge often becomes the focus of persuasive advocacy, and it should be antecedent to the act of debating. The questions for reflection may aid the student to test the mastery of the theory before proceeding to actually debate.

The second section provides moot legal cases which are efficacious in teaching students how to advocate persuasively. The murder cases are propositions of fact. They allow the student debater to organize three or four stock issues on the affirmative, likewise on the negative, and to develop a clash over a manageable amount of issues, evidence, and reasoning. The cases are constructed so that there is enough evidence to argue both sides of the given proposition, but without enough evidence to enable one side to clearly win over the opponent. In other words, if a win or clear verdict is desirable by the debaters, they will have to do a good job of selecting arguments and evidence for or against the proposition, rather than trying to amass evidence in an overkill fashion (the cases simply are not designed for or amenable to such a tactic). Thus, persuasive advocacy replaces the just-read-from-the-4x6-notecard mentality. The student debater should realize that the tests for evidence are built into the cases in order to test the debater's analytical powers in perceiving them and then proceeding to attack or defend the case by means of them. The winner, if so desired, is the debater who does the better job of persuasive advocacy on the proposition for the given case.

The time limits for these murder cases are flexible, and the individual instructor can introduce innovative formats as appropriate. Practice has indicated that constructive speeches from 6 to 8 minutes are optimal, and rebuttal speeches from 4 to 6 minutes are manageable. Sometimes two sets of rebuttals can help to teach students the mastery of this difficult type of speech. The debates are optimally done in Lincoln-Douglas style, one-on-one, but they can be disputed in team debating. The other members of the class may wish to serve as "jurors" of the debate.

These cases are especially helpful in teaching students the skills of direct and cross-examination. The list of testimony from several witnesses appended after the cases is specifically designed for that purpose. A prosecution and defense should conduct a practice direct and cross-examination period, and this may be done in round-robin fashion in order to give the student experience in both kinds of questioning. The debaters may then progress to calling witnesses (either by their own choice or by assignment) from the actual cases for the prosecution and the defense. A particular character from the case is role-played by a witness--chosen either from the class or from one's friends. The "witness" then responds to direct and cross-examination questions, as appropriate, from both the prosecution and the defense. Again, the manageability of the cases allows the questioner some control over the material in order to focus on the main task of building the requisite skills in the examination periods.

Lastly, these moot legal murder cases are fun but not frivolous to debate. The student debater should take the cases seriously because they are challenging to advocate; nevertheless, the cases are enjoyable to debate and to judge as an instructor. Each of the cases can be construed in a variety of interpretations, and debated with a choice of strategy and tactics. The bright and able student will occasionally invent a new case approach which may be devastating to the unprepared opponent and rewarding to the instructor who awaits a florescence of forensic genius. Pre-professional and pre-law students especially find the cases fascinating to advocate, and relevant to their speech communication needs in forensic advocacy.

PART I

CHAPTER ONE

A SHORT HISTORY OF DEBATE IN AMERICA

Debate has been, and continues to be, an important intellectual and political activity in the United States of America. Debate occurred in the colonial assemblies, in the writing of the Declaration of Independence, in the Constitutional Convention debates of 1787, and in the ensuing state ratification debates, of which Patrick Henry's and James Madison's of Virginia were prime examples. The slavery questions, debated in the Senate by such men as Webster, Clay, Calhoun, and Benton, captured listeners' attention on both sides of the Mason-Dixon line. Abraham Lincoln's series of debates across Illinois with Stephen Douglas made Lincoln famous, and these debates serve as the model for contemporary presidential debates, which began with Richard Nixon and John Kennedy in 1960. In the twentieth-century, presidents Theodore Roosevelt, Franklin Roosevelt, and Richard Nixon were debaters, and before he moved to the governorship of New Jersey and on to the Oval Office, Woodrow Wilson coached debate for a time at Princeton University. To this day, debate continues to draw students who become leaders in law, politics, and the professions.1 The history of the birth, rise, and practice of debate on the American college campus merits a closer examination.

Literary societies were the progenitors of contemporary academic debate. Picture a small campus in the eighteenth-century, often removed to rural areas in order to escape the vagaries of city life, on which there were few organized activities, athletics were unknown, and the dating of females on these all-male campuses was forbidden. There was little reading outside of a faculty approved list--often classical and religious in nature--so students felt a need to vent their energies and intellectual interests. They created their own debating clubs, called literary societies. These were the first extra-curricular student activities and organizations. The first one of these was the Spy Club at Harvard College, 1722. Yale had its Linonian Society, 1753; Princeton the American Whig in 1769 and the Cliosophic in 1770; Phi Beta Kappa was formed at the College of William and Mary in 1776; and Oberlin College had the first women's society in 1835, the

Young Ladies' Association. By the American Civil War, the literary societies were an integral part of student life, and remained the only sanctioned extra-curricular activity. Although the literary societies were idiosyncratic to the individual institutions, a common denominator was that a debate was held at each meeting. The following topics indicate the wide range of students' interests:

Yale, 1792, Whether women ought to be admitted to share in civil government.

Princeton, 1813, Are capital punishments beneficial or detrimental to a nation?

South Carolina, 1831, Should seduction be considered a capital crime?

Brown, 1854, Resolved, That the sale of ardent spirits ought to be prohibited by law.

Columbia, 1871, Resolved that all studies should be made elective during junior and senior years.

These topics were debated by members of the society within its confines, save for an occasional exhibition debate for the other students, faculty, and townspeople. But as early as 1830 at the University of Georgia, the Phi Beta Kappa society debated the Demosthenians, and the practice of intra-campus society debates spread to other schools. In 1881, Illinois College and Knox College met in what may have been the first inter-collegiate society debate, and other colleges quickly followed their lead.

The rise of modern intercollegiate, non-literary society, debating is dated from 1892 when Yale debated Harvard at Cambridge. By 1900, intercollegiate debating had spread among the eastern schools to midwestern schools such as Iowa, Minnesota, Wisconsin, Chicago, Illinois, and Ohio. Southern schools also formed debating leagues among themselves. Debaters sought aid in speaking from any likely professor, and by the first decade of 1900, one had in place a debate system easily recognizable today: a faculty debate "coach," the debate "squad," and often academic credit for intercollegiate debating. The 1920's witnessed the rise of international collegiate debating. Bates College went to Oxford in 1921, and the University of Oregon team literally toured around the world in 1927. The first modern debate tournament, with many schools attending, probably occurred at Southwestern College, Kansas, in 1923.

The kinds of debating practiced today have their traceable archetypes. One-on-one debating is usually termed Lincoln-Douglas, and it is geared toward developing and displaying individual debating prowess. The audience-style debate, in which the debate is decided by the entire audience rather than a single judge, evolved from the early exhibition debates of the literary societies and the early intercollegiate tournaments. Parliamentary style debating, modeled after the British union debating and characterized by wit and oratorical persuasion, is similar to audience-style debate, and like it, the decision is rendered by a division of the house. NDT-style debate, the acronym for the National Debate Tournament which produces in the spring of each year a national championship collegiate debate team, is judged by the debate coach-judge, who is skilled in the methodology and decision paradigms of that kind of debate. It evolved from the intercollegiate debate tournaments in the 1920's. CEDA-style debate, the acronym for the Cross Examination Debate Association, evolved from NDT-style debating with the major distinctions being reduced speaking times for the speeches--8 minute constructive speeches and 4 minute rebuttals vs. NDT's 10-5 format--and the nature of the resolution--NDT debaters dispute propositions of policy whereas CEDA debaters dispute propositions of value (these kinds of propositions will be discussed in the next chapter).

In summary, collegiate forensics has always appealed to students who wished to debate their ideas and beliefs, who enjoyed defending one's position and attacking the adversary's, and who wanted experience in persuading a critical judge or audience. The mastery of the art of argumentation and debate may allow the student debater to stand in the historical lineage of great Americans who attained excellence in debate and went on to obtain excellence in the world of law, letters, and legislation.

NOTES

[1]Ronald J. Matlon and Lucy M. Keele, "A Survey of Participants in the National Debate Tournament, 1947-1980," _Journal of the American Forensic Association_, 20 (1984), 194-205.

ADDITIONAL READINGS

Cowperthwaite, L. Leroy and Baird, A. Craig. "Intercollegiate Debating." _A History of Speech Education in America_. Ed. Karl R. Wallace. New York: Appleton-Century-Crofts, Inc., 1954.

Martel, Myles. _Political Campaign Debates: Images, Strategies, and Tactics_. New York: Longman Inc., 1983.

Potter, David. "The Literary Society." _A History of Speech Education in America_. Ed. Karl R. Wallace. New York: Appleton-Century-Crofts, Inc., 1954.

Ritter, Kurt. "Recapturing the Rhetorical Dimension: Debating in Campus Forums." _Speaker and Gavel_, 12 (1974), 1-3.

Wenzel, Joseph W. "Campus and Community Programs in Forensics: Needs and Opportunities." _Journal of the American Forensic Association_, 7 (1971), 253-59.

QUESTIONS FOR REFLECTION

1. Why did students form literary societies?

2. What are the various forms of academic debate today?

CHAPTER TWO

THE TERMINOLOGY OF DEBATE

Debate is an oral intellectual activity in which human discourse is adapted to certain given postulates and procedures. To be sure, debate can be conducted in written forms such as scholarly journals or popular periodicals, but for the purposes here, debate will be treated as an oral communication activity. But before proceeding to define the terms in debate, it is important to understand what comprises the debate situation.

In its simplest form, the debate situation consists of four important elements. First, it involves discourse, and often that discourse is dependent on the rules of debate terminology. Second, it involves concomitantly a speaker, or more than one, who perceives a need in society and who is motivated to satisfy that need through oral discourse. Third, it involves concomitantly another speaker who does not perceive the need and who is motivated to deny or contradict that need through speech. So far, only two opposing speakers exist, they are not yet debaters; therefore, the fourth element is critical: both speakers must agree to let a third party judge the debate. Hereinafter, judge will be used in a generic sense, but one will remember that the judge can be an audience of one to many persons. For an illustration of the debate situation, Abraham Lincoln tried to make the spread of slavery an issue in the 1858 senatorial race in Illinois, Stephen Douglas did not think Southern slavery should be an issue in Illinois politics; and both agreed to give a series of debates before the voters of Illinois who would act as judge. Similar debate situations exist in the lawcourts, in the various kinds of arbitration, in legislative bodies, in political candidates' debates, and in the various forms of academic debate.

The special names of discourse in debate correspond to the functions and responsibilities of the two speakers. The debater who seeks to satisfy a need is the affirmative and delivers an affirmative speech. In the courtroom, the affirmative is the plaintiff or the prosecuting attorney. The debater who denies the need is the negative and gives a negative speech, and the negative is the defendant or the defense attorney. The nature of the need must be nominated in nomenclature, and that language is called a proposition or resolution. A proposition may be defined as a need expressed in a declarative sentence. For instance, "Resolved: That X is guilty of the murder of Y" communicates the need to determine the fact or not of X's guilt; "Resolved: That General Lee was a better general than General Grant" expresses the need to ascertain the relative value of their respective generalships; likewise, "Resolved: That the U.S.A. should abolish nuclear armaments" communicates a need to adopt a new policy. Therefore, the debate situation may now be defined as one in which affirmative and negative speakers present opposing discourses on a proposition before a judge. With an understanding of the rudiments of the debate situation in hand, the special terminology which operates in it may be discussed.

STATUS QUO is Latin and literally means the state which, or more commonly, the state existing. The status quo is a term which refers to existing institutions, governments, mores, and laws. The status quo is not necessarily or logically better or worse than that which was or could be, it just describes what is. Before Martin Luther nailed his 95 Theses for debate on the door at Wittenburg in the early sixteenth-century, the Roman Catholic Church was the religion of the status quo in Europe; after Luther, many different religions became the status quo throughout the continent. The status quo is a descriptive, but not an evaluative, term. The negative defends the status quo.

PRESUMPTION takes the concept of the status quo one step further. Presumption is a rule of debate, and it may be defined as the ground of reasonable belief which stands good until sufficient reason is presented against it. Without putting too fine a point upon it, presumption is evaluative in a qualitative sense. "A man is presumed innocent until proven guilty" is an example of presumption in American jurisprudence. This presumption places a certain evaluation on the status quo, which, by rule, we say must stand true until proven otherwise. Since the negative defends the status quo, the negative has presumption in its favor. Since the presumption suggests a certain qualitative evaluation, a reasonable question follows, "How much proof does it take to remove or 'overcome' presumption?" That question can be answered by addressing the next term.

6

BURDEN OF PROOF may be defined as the duty to prove the proposition. The Latin for burden of proof, onus probandi, literally means the burden, duty, or charge of proving. Notice that in discharging the burden or duty, an appreciable amount of reasoning and analysis is produced to overcome the positive evaluation of presumption. The degree at which the affirmative's arguments, comprising the burden of proof, dislodge the negative presumption is called "beyond a reasonable doubt." The affirmative must prove beyond a reasonable doubt the proposition. Precisely where the locus of the "beyond" is, is often disputed in the debate. Ultimately, the judge decides the locus of "beyond" a reasonable doubt when the debate decision is rendered. Still, the important point is that the affirmative has a appreciable burden of proof, although it is incapable of being exactly measured, to prove beyond a reasonable doubt the resolution.

The onus probandi is by rule assigned to the affirmative, which has presumption against it. The burden of proof lies always with the affirmative, it never changes or shifts during the debate because the affirmative always has the duty to prove the proposition. By examining the next term, the burden of proof can be more precisely described and its substance more fully developed.

The PRIMA FACIE CASE derives from the Latin, prima facie, which means on first appearance or at first sight. The prima facie case may be defined as that case which a reasonable judge would allow to prevail until contradicted and overcome by a counter case. Case means the best corpus of reasons and analysis and evidence which the affirmative and negative can each muster. The affirmative discharges its burden of proof in the prima facie case: on first appearance or hearing by the judge, the case seems to prevail against the presumption of the status quo. By rule of debate, certain proofs must be presented in the prima facie case, and these will be explained later. Before proceeding, a recapitulation is expedient. The affirmative perceives a need in the status quo, and delineates it in the prima facie case, thus discharging the burden of proof. The negative is motivated to speak against the affirmative attack because it, at first sight, was strong enough--if left undenied--to warrant a verdict against the status quo and the negative. As the affirmative has the onus probandi, so does the negative have a burden which is examined next.

7

BURDEN OF REBUTTAL. If the affirmative presents a prima facie case, then the negative is obliged to go forward with the debate. The burden of rebuttal may be defined as the onus of refuting the opposing case. As the debate unfolds, the negative first has the burden of rebuttal against the affirmative. But the burden of rebuttal then shifts back and forth as the debate further unfolds. After the negative discharges its burden of rebuttal in its first speech of the debate, then the affirmative has the burden of rebuttal to refute the negative's case and to defend the prima facie case, and so it goes, back and forth, until the time limit expires or the agreed-upon number of speeches have been delivered to the judge. Thus, two important points to remember in a debate are (1) that the affirmative always has the burden of proof throughout the debate to prove the proposition, and (2) that the affirmative and negative both have have the burden of rebuttal--the responsibility to refute each other's cases.

At this point, attention is returned to the proposition, a need expressed in a declarative sentence, in order to understand the vital relationship between the proposition, the burden of proof, and the prima facie case. The proposition serves three functions:

1. To serve as the basis for dispute in the debate by describing the need in language;

2. To place correctly the burden of proof with the affirmative and the presumption with the negative;

3. To indicate the nature of the prima facie case.

Since the affirmative determines the language of the resolution, it has the obligation and the right to define the terms in the proposition. The following are guidelines in defining terms:

1. It is not necessary to define every word, but only those words which are new, ambiguous, or critical to understanding the prima facie case.

2. Use authoritative sources such as standard dictionaries or legal dictionaries [Black's Legal Dictionary, for example].

3. Define the terms objectively and fairly.

The debater should realize that a sly affirmative could so define the terms in the proposition, so "load" the language, that the affirmative case would be virtually assured a positive verdict. As a function of the burden of rebuttal in such an instance, the negative has a right and responsibility to object to the judge--by denying the affirmative's definitions using the criteria above--in order to have the judge decide the debate on the objection alone (but usually there are other issues which the negative will additionally want to deny).

Three kinds of propositions are generally recognized. First is a proposition of fact which alleges the existence of a thing, a need, etc. For instance, "The Soviets break treaties" and "Acid rain exists" are examples of propositions of fact. Next are propositions of value which express evaluative assessments about a fact without recommending a course of action. From the two sample propositions of fact above, the affirmative might additionally perceive a new need by resolving that "The Soviet's breaking of treaties is bad" or "Acid rain harms trees." Finally, propositions of policy assert a need for a new course of action or a change in present policy: "The federal government should reduce the emissions of acid rain" or "The U.S.A. should not sign further treaties with the Soviets."

Notice that a proposition of fact is the basic foundation of the need (if no need exists, then there is no logical reason to proceed to value and policy); a proposition of value builds on a need (if the value is not "bad," then there is no logical reason to proceed to policy); and a proposition of policy builds on the previous affirmation of fact and value (if the policy is negated, it could be interpreted two-fold: nothing at all should be done, or a new policy, different from the first one advocated, should be advanced for consideration, etc.).

Propositions have, by rule, issues which are germane to their genre. An issue may be defined as that question or point in dispute which the affirmative must prove or the entire affirmative case must fall. The prima facie case usually consists of several issues, and all of them must be proved or the whole case fails. Propositions of policy have by rule three stock issues

9

in the prima facie case: a Need, a Plan or policy to
satisfy the Need, and a demonstration of how the Plan-
Meets-the-Need. There would be no rational reason to
propose a policy without a need, nor would one accept a
plan until convinced that it would indeed solve the
problem. The issues in propositions of value are not
so clear-cut or amenable to determination by rule;
rather, they logically ensue from the very language of
the proposition, and hence the selection of the issues
may become an issue in the debate. In the value
proposition "General Lee was a better general than
General Grant," the need is to determine the charac-
teristics of a "better" general. How the affirmative
defines those terms inescapably determines its issues
in the prima facie case. In propositions of fact, the
issues can flow out of the very language of the
resolution, as they do in value ones, or they can be
stipulated by rule. For instance, and especially in
terms of the moot legal cases presented in Part II, the
stock issues in second-degree murder are Motive, Means,
and Presence [find their meanings in a legal
dictionary]. Notice that even if the affirmative could
prove X had a motive and means to kill Y, but that the
negative could disprove presence, then the entire prima
facie case would fail because the prosecution was unable to affirm the vital issue of presence; likewise,
the issues for first-degree murder are Motive, Means,
Presence, and Premeditation.

By definition, issues can be subdivided into their
classes. Actual issues are the questions arising from
the prima facie case. From time to time, the negative
may wish to acquiesce in an issue, and this is called
an admitted issue. To the extent that the negative admits an issue--due to the absence of compelling reasoning and analysis--that does help the affirmative's
prima facie case, but the negative need not spend valuable time on an issue it has very little probability of
winning. The actual issues minus the admitted issues
(if any) equal the contested issues. These are the vital issues in contest or disputation, and the affirmative must carry all of the contested issues in order
to win the debate (if the negative admits an issue, it
automatically goes to the affirmative).

At last, the stage is set to state the manner in
which the judge should decide a debate. There are two
rules for a verdict. First, was a prima facie case
established? In the courtroom, the defense attorney
might say, "Your honor, we move a dismissal of the

case. The prosecution has not presented a prima facie case," before beginning even to defend the client. If the judge finds for the defense, the debate stops there; otherwise, the defense must proceed with the burden of rebuttal. In the classroom debate, the student debater would certainly want to communicate to the judge the negative's belief that the affirmative did not present a prima facie case, which, if true, would by itself indicate a negative verdict. But ordinarily, the negative would continue to debate in order to gain practice and to protect itself lest the judge believed there was a prima facie case presented. The second rule is, did the affirmative maintain a preponderance of proof--proof beyond a reasonable doubt--on the contested issues? If, in the judge's opinion, the affirmative did prove all of the contested issues beyond a reasonable doubt, then the affirmative would win; if the negative prevailed on one or more issues, even one is enough, then the affirmative case would fail and the negative would win.

QUESTIONS FOR REFLECTION

1. What are the four elements of the debate situation?

2. What is the status quo?

3. What is presumption and what side has it?

4. What is the onus probandi and what side has it?

5. What is the burden of rebuttal? Can it change?

6. What is the prima facie case? Who has it?

7. What is a proposition? What kinds are there? Who defines it?

8. What are issues? What kinds are there?

9. What are the two rules for deciding a debate?

CHAPTER THREE

ARGUMENTATION, PERSUASION, AND EVIDENCE

At the outset, the debater needs to appreciate the similarities and differences between argumentation and persuasion in order to practice successfully the art of persuasive advocacy; accordingly, persuasion and argumentation must be compared and contrasted.

Not all persuasive speakers are debaters nor are all debaters persuasive speakers, yet there is a certain sense in which being a persuasive speaker can make one a better debater, and being a good debater can make one a better persuasive speaker. Around 320 B.C., Aristotle defined the art of persuasive speaking as "the faculty of observing in any given situation the available means of persuasion."[1] The speaker had to know how to make the listener believe the orator credible (_ethos_), how to stir the hearer's emotions (_pathos_), and how to prove the truth or apparent truth of an argument (_logos_). While the debater should always remember that emotional and ethical appeals function to persuade the judge in any debate, there is a certain sense in which the debater pays special attention to proving the truth or apparent truth in the debate situation. Argumentation is closely identified with _logos_ or reasoned discourse. The ken of the debater is generally associated primarily with logical argumentation, whereas the persuader tends to utilize all three of the means of persuasion. Argumentation occurs in a distinct debate situation, with two opposing speakers addressing a judge, as juxtaposed to the persuasive situation which usually involves only one speaker talking to a judge. In the debate situation, there are affirmative and negative debaters, and one of them is perceived by the judge to be more believable or persuasive. Why the judge believes one is more persuasive than the other is the subject and focus of this chapter.

Argumentation may be defined as the process of trying to present a persuasive proof. The process begins when the debater perceives a need which would be changed through discourse in the debate situation. The second step begins when the debater gathers evidence which supports the need. Evidence may be defined as the reason for belief. Note that although the debater might believe the evidence is a reason for belief (and it might _be_ so in a Platonic sense), the evidence really functions as "evidence" only if the judge believes it. For instance, the combination of a dead body with a knife in the corpse would be perceived as evidence--grounds for belief--that a murder was committed; but on the basis of just that evidence alone, one could just as easily infer and hence argue suicide. When enough evidence is gathered, the debater ends the second step by framing the language of the proposition from that evidence: "X is guilty of the murder of Y." The third step involves testing the veracity of the proposition. The process involves identifying and evaluating all of the relevant evidence which either supports or denies the proposition. In this step, the debater will select the best evidence for the case, and be prepared to refute troublesome and contradictory evidence [how to do that will be presented in the last section of this chapter]. The fourth and final step is to present the evidence in oral advocacy. With the process of argumentation posited, attention can now be focused on the substance of argumentation.

Arguments are the substance of advocacy. An argument may be defined as a reason or reasons for something. In the debate situation, an affirmative and negative offer different and sometimes diametrically opposed arguments to support or deny the proposition. But what is that "something" of the above definition? It is evidence. In other words, an argument is the reasonable language which the debater employs to make the evidence, the ground for belief, credible or persuasive. The end of argumentation is proof, but what is the connection between evidence, argument, and proof?

Proof may be defined as evidence so convincing so as to demonstrate a conclusion beyond a reasonable doubt. Unfortunately, the real-world is generally an inhospitable environment in which to find evidence which meets that strict definition; rather, the debater usually finds evidence which approaches or approximates that strict standard. That is why people debate: people do not perceive the "evidence" in the same fashion, and to the extent of their difference, therein lies the focus of the disputation. It is the debater's function to offer reasons--arguments--for making evidence a proof. Notice that the judge decides with what side the preponderance of proof lies. Notice that the decision is based on not what really or actually is, but on what the judge believes is. That is why "innocent" people are sometimes convicted, why "bad" policies are enacted, and why sometimes "guilty" people go free, and "good" policies are not enacted. In order to make evidence be persuasive, the debater needs to know how to argue or how to use language to construct a persuasive proof. An understanding, mastery, and application of the classification and tests of evidence will aid in making the debater a persuasive advocate, so attention is directed first to classifying evidence, and then how to argue the tests of evidence.

ORIGINAL or HEARSAY. Original evidence consists of data based on first-hand sense perception, "I heard X say he hated Y." On the other hand, hearsay evidence is second-hand information, once removed from the reporter. "M told me that she heard X say he hated Y" is hearsay evidence. Generally speaking, it is less reliable and often inadmissible evidence because if M were unavailable for questioning, the hearsay evidence could not be verified. The debater should object to hearsay evidence in most instances.

DIRECT or CIRCUMSTANTIAL. Direct evidence exists in the form of facts, statistics, statements, objects, etc. These forms directly or straightforwardly affirm a ground for belief. A knife in a corpse is direct evidence which supports a reasonable ground for believing that the knife was the instrument of death. On the other hand, circumstantial evidence indicates an indirect inference, it does not directly affirm a point. Based on the circumstances above, one could argue that the knife was the decedent's, and hence, it was a matter of suicide; or that is was X's knife, hence it was a matter of murder. Before the advent of fingerprinting, and absent any positive identification of the knife, both of those arguments are reasonable. They could be proved only by searching for other kinds of direct or circumstantial evidence which illuminate the need. Whenever possible, the debater should try to support and corroborate circumstantial evidence with direct evidence. To the extent that one's opponent does not do that, then the debater should object to drawing the opponent's conclusions from such evidence.

PREAPPOINTED or CASUAL. Preappointed evidence is created or preserved for specific purposes for being used later as evidence. Examples of this type are wills, contracts, licenses, laws, etc. Casual evidence is not uttered, written, or preserved for any particular reason to be used later as evidence. Both kinds of evidence have their strengths and weaknesses. Just as one could preappoint a true or false statement or document, so too could one casually tell a truth or falsehood.

EAGER or RELUCTANT. Eager evidence appears to work toward the source's or reporter's advantage. On the face of it, one would be naturally wary of eager evidence, but that does not imply that it is necessarily bad or weak. On the other hand, reluctant evidence appears to work against the source's or the reporter's advantage; consequently, on the face of it, reluctant evidence should have a greater probative value than eager evidence. The debater should communicate the existence, or lack thereof, of the higher probative evidence.

POSITIVE or NEGATIVE. Positive evidence directly affirms a point or contention, whereas negative evidence is the absence of positive evidence to the contrary. The problem of negative evidence ensues from the certainty of the "absence." How does one prove nihility? For example, "How do you know a fish cannot climb a tree? Did you ever see one not do it?" Since one doubtlessly has not, can one maintain a fish can climb a tree? However, there are circumstances wherein one can adduce a ground for belief on the basis of a lack of evidence to the contrary. If the debater will refer back to the knife example above, the statement "the absence of any positive identification of the knife" is an example of negative evidence. If no one could identify the knife, and no one could say that Y owned the knife, the absence of evidence to the contrary would give a reasonable ground to conclude it was not Y's knife. That assumption may or may not indicate that the knife was X's (it could be Z's, etc.). Notice that positive evidence is more believable than negative evidence, but that general observation does not always obtain in all circumstances.

Before leaving the classifications, it may be efficacious to indicate that a unit or piece of evidence can exist concomitantly in different classifications. For illustration, "M saw X have a gun" is original, direct, casual, positive, and--if M were X's brother-- reluctant. "N never saw X have a gun" is original, direct, but based on negative evidence. With these classifications in mind, it is appropriate to investigate the tests for evidence, and how to argue them.

15

EXPERT or LAYMAN. Generally speaking, expert testimony, which is based on the reporter's training and expertise in the matter at issue, is preferable to lay testimony. But might expert evidence be too eager? preappointed? circumstantial? Therein is the argument.

RELEVANT or IRRELEVANT. The degree to which evidence addresses or sustains a point should be ascertained. Relevance arises from the situation and is determined by the final proof which one wishes to make. For instance, it might appear irrelevant whether a hunter, who was shot by another hunter, wore camouflaged clothing or blaze orange vestments. But if one suspected murder, the prior question of the color of the clothing could be very relevant if one wished to ascertain how easily the victim could be spotted in a forest: was it an accident or on purpose. It might at first appear irrelevant which way a knife blade was positioned in a corpse; but if one knew that the deceased was right-handed and that the knife blade pointed toward the left half of the body, what might be a reasonable and very relevant inference one could make?

OLD or NEW. Usually, old evidence is subject to the vicissitudes of the elements and of the human memory, whereas new evidence is more likely to be pristine and fresh. Could new preappointed evidence be suspect? Could new reluctant evidence be more credible than old eager evidence? Those are possible lines of argumentation.

PLANTED. One needs to be aware that evidence could be so placed or positioned so as to mislead purposefully the perceiver. One could plant original or hearsay evidence, plant direct or circumstantial evidence, etc. Planted evidence could be an insidious form of preappointed evidence.

BIAS. Bias is the internal motivation for a reporter to give evidence, knowingly or unknowingly, which is slanted or tilted, to whatever degree, from the "truth." The debater needs to determine the bias of the reporter in order to detract from the credibility of the source. In eager evidence, is the bias egregious? Attacking bias is a strong argument against that evidence.

LYING. Reporters or sources lie. When there are direct contradictions between X's and Y's testimony, it

16

is obvious that one of them is absolutely lying, or
that both of them are lying to some degree. Yet, lies
are hard to detect and difficult to prove, but the
classifications and other tests for evidence may aid in
the determination of a lie, or determining the truth.

INTERNAL and EXTERNAL CONSISTENCY. This is probably
the most important test of evidence. Internal consistency means that all of X's testimony is consistent,
agrees, holds together in its entirety. If X's testimony has inconsistencies in it, one could reasonably
conclude that X was lying, extremely biased, or perhaps
relied on hearsay, circumstantial, or negative
evidence. Internally consistent evidence is obviously
more credible than inconsistent evidence. External
consistency refers to the fact the X's testimony
(itself internally consistent) agrees with,
corroborates, sustains Y's testimony (itself internally
consistent) so that both are said to be externally
consistent. X's and Y's internally and externally consistent testimony would probably have more probative
value than O's internally consistent, but contradictory
to X's and Y's, testimony (O could be a consistent
liar). Would the fact that X and Y are laymen versus
the expert E, or that their testimony was old versus
E's being new, affect the ground for belief?

Summary

     Evidence is the crucial ground for persuasion.
But because evidence as evidence usually does not stand
alone as sufficient ground for belief--or there would
be no reason to dispute over evidence--the debater must
use oral advocacy to make the evidence appear more or
less credible to the judge. That persuasive advocacy
depends first on the debater's understanding of the
classifications and tests for evidence. Then the
debater proves or disproves the truth or apparent truth
(logos) of the argument by showing the strengths or
weaknesses of the evidence via the classifications and
tests. The debater applies the appropriate classifications and tests to the specific evidence at hand,
and clearly demonstrates to the judge that the evidence
at dispute should be believed because it is recent expert testimony, etc., or that it is not worthy of
belief because it is a lie, or internally
contradictory, etc. Hence, the argument, which the
evidence supports, should be accepted or rejected. In
the next chapter, this process of persuasive argumentation will be placed in a practical how-to-do-it

perspective.

NOTES

[1]Aristotle, _Rhetoric_, trans. W. Rhys Roberts (New York: The Modern Library, 1954), $1355_{b}26$.

ADDITIONAL READINGS

Harte, Thomas B. "Audience Ability to Apply Tests of Evidence." _Journal of the American Forensic Asso-_, _ciation_, 8 (1971), 109-15.

Newman, Robert P. and Newman, Dale R. _Evidence_. Boston: Houghton Mifflin Co., 1969.

Nizer, Louis. _My Life in Court_. New York: Doubleday and Co., 1961.

_____. _Thinking on Your Feet_. New York: Liveright Publishing Co., 1940.

QUESTIONS FOR REFLECTION

1. What are _pathos_, _ethos_, and _logos_?

2. What is argumentation?

3. What is an argument?

4. What is proof?

5. What are the classifications of evidence?

6. Where applicable, which ones of these are more credible?

7. What are the tests for evidence?

8. Where appropriate, which ones of these are more probative?

CHAPTER FOUR

THE PRACTICE OF DEBATE

In this chapter, the theory of persuasive argumentation is applied to the practice of debate. In Section One, an outlined illustration will be given for three sample affirmative cases on propositions of fact, value, and policy. The proposition and the issues comprising the prima facie case will be given for each kind, but the substructure of the supporting evidence and argument will be excluded (the substructure may be examined more closely in the Johnson Case sample affirmative speech and brief). In Section Two, the approaches to negative case construction will be discussed and outlined in terms of the negative's burden of rebuttal to the three affirmative cases. Section Three will carry the debate forward by illustrating an affirmative rebuttal and a negative rebuttal for each of the sample cases. Section Four will explain and illustrate the important argumentative process of attack and defense. Section Five will conclude by treating direct and cross-examination. Throughout the sections, it is hoped that the continuity of the three constant case examples will make the art of debating clear and comprehensible.

Section One: Building the Affirmative Case

The affirmative prima facie case is constructed from the issues inherent in the proposition. The three kinds of propositions will be treated in their turn.

Proposition of Fact: "X is guilty of the first degree murder of Y."

   I. X had the means to kill Y.
  II. X had the presence to kill Y.
 III. X had the motive to kill Y.
 IV. X premeditated the murder of Y.

Under the appropriate issue, the affirmative assembles all of the relevant evidence and argument which supports that issue. This analysis can be outlined in the traditional A., 1., a., substructure format (see the sample Johnson brief and outline).

Proposition of Value: "General Lee was a better general than General Grant."

19

I. General Lee was a better tactician.
II. General Lee was a gentlemanly soldier.
III. General Lee instilled personal allegiance in his soldiers.

The debater would want to define what "better" and "general" meant in order to support those issues with historical evidence, and perhaps with lay and expert testimony. Can you think of more appropriate issues to support the proposition?

Proposition of Policy: "The federal government should reduce the emissions of acid rain."

I. Acid rain exists.
II. Acid rain is harmful.
III. The Plan, the federal government shall
A. Monitor emissions at a safe standard.
B. Invoke fines and imprisonment for violators.
IV. The Plan will allow the federal government to reduce the emissions of acid rain.

The affirmative would need to define the terms of the proposition as necessary, and present the best available evidence for proof.

Section Two: Building the Negative Case

In discharging the burden of rebuttal, the negative may select from three options. These strategies are a defense of the status quo, pure refutation, and the counterplan or counterproposal. While the counterproposal is a distinct strategy with certain possibilities and limitations in its application, the negative will often utilize in an actual debate some agreeable mix of pure refutation and defense of the status quo; nevertheless, these two options are distinct enough to separate them for individual discussion.

Defense of the Status Quo. The negative stance in this option is defensive, it argues that the status quo is worth defending in its own right, and it alleges that the negative's position is secure against assault. The defense of the status quo is a posture wherein the negative asks the judge to compare and contrast the prima facie case with the defense of the status quo as the more convincing argumentative "reality" than the affirmative's prima facie case argument of it.

The negative has two tactics to argue, and these ensue from Cicero's conception of stasis in argument.1 Stasis denotes where the argument clashes. The negative can argue the stases of fact (_conjecturalis_) and/or definition (_definitiva_). For instance, a defense attorney could adduce new and different facts to defend the client and/or argue that the facts at dispute should be defined or viewed in a new or different manner. Against the prosecution's witnesses who testify that X was present at the murder, the defense may introduce witnesses who vouch for X's alibi; or while admitting that X was present, the defense could argue the stasis of definition that although X was present, X was not there for the purpose of committing murder. Thus, the negative marshals the evidence and argument which support, in a straightforward fashion, the status quo. In its truest sense, the defense of the status quo is a strategy, through the two tactics of clashing on fact and/or definition, to lay out the arguments in a constructive fashion to defend the status quo, and it therefore pays little attention to attacking directly the affirmative prima facie case but rather supports the negative stand. In actual debating, the defense of the status quo, in its pure state, is a relatively rare negative stance. More than likely, it is usually linked symbiotically to the next strategy.

Pure Refutation. In juxtaposition to the defense of the status quo, pure refutation is offensive, it attacks the affirmative's prima facie case, it denies the affirmative's evidence and argument. Notice that the negative could confute the affirmative's prima facie case through pure refutation without ever recurring to defending the status quo or one's client; however, depending on the debate situation, a combination of defense and refutation may be the most advantageous alternative. The stance or strategy of pure refutation is denial, it asserts the untruth of stated evidence or argument. Pure refutation is accomplished by attacking or denying the affirmative's evidence and/or argument. Since Chapter Three has explicated the classifications and tests for evidence--which are the bases of pure refutation--it would be redundant to repeat them here; therefore, how the negative debater can attack the affirmative's argument will be examined next.

In pure refutation, the negative denies the argument, or the reason for something, by negating the affirmative's analysis or reasoning. As for the

21

analysis, the negative may deny the affirmative's definition of terms or its selection of issues (these were fully discussed in Chapter Two). It is left, then, to explicate how the negative can deny the affirmative's reasoning.

A mistaken argument or reasoning is called a fallacy, wherein the process of inference is incorrect. A fallacy is a defect in proof and a faulty argument which appears, at first sight, to be persuasive, but upon closer examination it does not warrant the claim it asserts. Here follow the kinds of fallacious arguments.

Argumentum ad vercundiam is an unwarranted appeal to authority, and is sometimes called the "Honorable Chinese Ancestors" argument as if age and authorities of whatever type are always and necessarily to be believed. In the Congressional debates over the Compromise of 1850, John Calhoun wisely objected to Northerners' appealing to the name and honor of George Washington in an effort to save the Union: "Nor can the Union be saved by invoking the name of the illustrious Southerner whose mortal remains repose on the western bank of the Potomac. He was one of us--a slaveholder and a planter."2 During a debate in Faneuil Hall in 1837 over resolutions to condemn the murder of Rev. Elijah Lovejoy in Alton, Illinois, Wendell Phillips appealed to honorable American ancestors: "Sir, when I heard the gentleman lay down principles which place the murderers of Alton by the side of Otis and Hancock, with Quincy and Adams, I thought those pictured lips [pointing to the portraits in the Hall] would have broken into voice to rebuke the recreant American, -- the slanderer of the dead."3

Argumentum ad misericordiam is an appeal to pity, sometimes termed softening the audience. Clarence Darrow used the fallacy effectively in his own self-defense in 1912: "There are people who would destroy me. There are people who would lift up their hands to crush me down. I have enemies powerful and strong."4

Argumentum ad populum, often termed "appealing to the gallery" or to the people, is an appeal to popular sentiment and belief irrespective of the facts at hand. Huey Long, playing to popular beliefs, erroneously argued that the money in the United States was owned by a very few rich persons: "When you have a country where one man owns more than 100,000 people, or a million people, and when you have a country where there are four men, as in America, that have got more control over things than all the 120,000,000 people together, you know what the trouble is."5

Argumentum ad hominem is an appeal to the base motives and personal interests and considerations of the audience. Abraham Lincoln used this argument in appealing to the racial prejudices of his audience in his debate with Stephen Douglas at Alton, Illinois, in 1858: "We profess to have no taste for running and catching niggers--at least, I profess no taste for that job at all."6

Argumentum ad personam is a personal attack on one's opponent, often illustrated by "If one has no case, then abuse your opponent." Joseph McCarthy spoke a classic example in his "Red-Tinted Washington Crowd" speech [which title is even an example of argumentum ad personam] when he attacked President Harry Truman: "Truman, I think, essentially, while a cheap little politician, is a loyal American"; and on the floor of the United States Senate, McCarthy maligned Secretary of State Dean Acheson: "When this pompous diplomat in striped pants, with a phony British accent, proclaimed to the American people that Christ on the Mount endorsed communism, high treason, and betrayal of a sacred trust, the blasphemy was so great that it awakened the dormant indignation of the American people."7

Argumentum ad crenam is an unwarranted appeal to the purse or wallet. "It costs too much" or "We cannot afford it" or "It will bankrupt the country" are familiar examples.

Argumentum ad ignorantiam uses the lack of proof to sustain an argument, as in "Since no one can prove otherwise, communication with the dead is possible."

Argumentum ad baculum, using the big stick, is an appeal to fear or to force. William Yancey made an appeal to force at the Democratic national convention in 1860 in a debate over a positive slave code in the Territories of the United States: "Let them see that there will be disunion. Do you urge upon them that there will be disunion if we are defeated."8

Petitio principii is begging the question, or arguing in a circle. The arguer erroneously demonstrates

a conclusion via a premise which assumes that
conclusion. In his "My Side of the Story" speech,
Richard Nixon begged the question: "Let me say this:
I don't believe that I ought to quit because I am not a
quitter."9

Non sequitur, it does not follow, is erroneous because it bases a conclusion on an insufficient or wrong
reason. Robert Thornwell, a Southern clergyman, tried
to argue that Negroes were slaves because of sin:
"Slavery is a part of the curse which sin has intro-
duced into the world, and stands in the same general
relations to Christianity as poverty, sickness, disease
or death."10 The argument is insufficient and wrong
because since whites sinned, too, why were they not
slaves, too?

Post hoc ergo propter hoc, after this, therefore,
because of this, is faulty because a cause for one
thing is incorrectly assumed as a cause of another.
The core argument of Abraham Lincoln's famous "House
Divided" speech in 1858 is a good example of this
fallacy. Lincoln argued that the conspiracy between
two Presidents, the Supreme Court, and Senator Douglas
--which conspiracy was the supposed cause for the Dred
Scott decision--was now the cause for the apparent conspiracy to make all of the free states in the Union
slave states by a second Dred Scott-like decision. Of
course, the evidence for both of these "causes" was
very fragile and suspect.11

Reductio ad absurdam, or reduction to absurdity,
occurs when the arguer extends the argument beyond its
intended application. An argument is taken to its
logical and absurd conclusion in order to demonstrate
the invalidity of the initial argument. Henry Clay
argued reductio ad absurdam effectively in his debate
over the Compromise of 1850 by applying the seces-
sionist doctrine to its logical consequence: "But how
are you going to separate them? . . . we should begin
at least with three confederacies--the Confederacy of
the North, the Confederacy of the Atlantic Southern
States, and the Confederacy of the Valley of the
Mississippi. . . . But other confederacies would spring
up. . . . There would be the Confederacy of the Lakes--
perhaps the Confederacy of New England and of the
Middle States."12

While these fallacies are included in this section
of how to build the negative case, with particular

regard to pure refutation, it is extremely important for the debater to note that these fallacies can be used just as easily and erroneously by the negative as by the affirmative; therefore, the affirmative has an opportunity and an obligation to object to their utilization by the negative, just as the negative may object to the affirmative's employment of the fallacies. In debate, at least, turn about is fair play.

Further, in an attempt to refute the affirmative's reasoning, the negative may object to the employment of special argumentative devices. Of course, these devices could be erroneously employed by the negative; accordingly, the affirmative would want to object to their usage, too.

The first one of these special devices is termed turning-the-tables. Therein, the debater takes an argument, made by the opponent in support of the opponent's case, and turns it back on the opponent in order to demonstrate how that argument actually harms the opponent's case! John Calhoun turned-the-tables on his Northern adversaries, when they argued that the South should follow the patriotic example of George Washington, by demonstrating that Washington had advocated and led a revolution against an oppressive government.12

Amphiboly is a device which notes ambiguous sentence construction. For instance, "We heard praise of angels" could mean we heard people praising angels, or it could mean that the angels themselves were doing the praising. Other examples are: "Homemakers: save soap and waste paper [is 'waste' an adjective or a verb?]," "Respectable entertainment every night but Sunday [is the entertainment disrespectable on Sunday?]," and "Rugby takes leather balls."

A third device is known as loaded words, wherein the technique is to use suggestive emotional connotations of devil or god terms in order to short-circuit the reasoning process. Typical examples are: un-American, hand-outs, the American way, creeping liberalism, knee-jerk reactionaries, welfare queens, revenue enhancement, etc.

Another device is posing a dilemma, or sometimes known as the horns of a dilemma. One presents the opponent with two argumentative choices so that the

25

proverbial two-edged Damoclean sword will cut down the opponent's reasoning on either position or horn. Lincoln tellingly used this device on Douglas in their debate at Alton when Lincoln argued that popular sovereignty had squatted out of existence, but if Douglas advocated the concept of unfriendly police laws to slavery, then Douglas was in reality arguing against the Constitution which expressly recognized slavery and the right of Southerners to have their fugitive slaves returned.13

The fifth, and last, device is the straw man or straw issues. This occurs when an arguer sets up pretended or straw men issues, and then proceeds to refute or knock them down easily, as one would demolish a scarecrow. The arguer picks the issues which are easily won. John Kennedy accused, in effect, Richard Nixon of using straw issues in the 1960 presidential debates when Kennedy alleged: "So that really isn't an issue in this campaign. It isn't an issue with Mr. Nixon, who now says he also supports the Eisenhower policy. Nor is the question that all Americans want peace and security an issue in this campaign. The question is: Are we moving in the direction of peace and security? Is our relative strength growing?"14

Here follows "Noodle's Oration," so-called because only a noodle-brain would give such a speech. This synthetic speech was composed by Sydney Smith, an Anglican clergyman, in 1825. It contains all of the fallacies and special devices discussed above. The speech is supposedly set in a debate in the British Parliament, but the keen debater will note that the speech could advocate or refute almost any proposition or subject in almost any setting. The contained fallacies and devices appear to be persuasive at first glance (how many times have you heard similar sentiments offered?), but if one criticizes the speech carefully, and has some fun in the process, then one will perceive how silly the argument actually is, and probably have the fun Smith had in writing "Noodle's Oration." The text is from The Edinburgh Review, 42 (August, 1825), 386-89.

NOODLE'S ORATION

"What would our ancestors say to this, Sir? How does this measure tally with their institutions? How does it agree with their experience? Are we to put the wisdom of yesterday in competition with the wisdom of

centuries? [Hear! Hear!] Is beardless youth to show
no respect for the decisions of mature age? [Loud
cries of Hear! Hear!] If this measure be right, would
it have escaped the wisdom of those Saxon progenitors
to whom we are indebted for so many of our best political institutions? Would the Dane have passed it over?
Would the Norman have rejected it? Would such a
notable discovery have been reserved for these modern
and degenerate times? Besides, Sir, if the measure itself is good, I ask the honourable gentleman if this
is the time for carrying it into execution--whether, in
fact, a more unfortunate period could have been
selected than that which he has chosen? If this were
an ordinary measure, I should not oppose it with so
much vehemence; but, Sir, it calls in question the wisdom of an irrevocable law--of a law passed at the
memorable period of the Revolution. What right have
we, Sir, to break down this firm column, on which the
great men of that day stamped a character of eternity?
Are not all authorities against this measure--Pitt,
Fox, Cicero, and the Attorney and Solicitor General?
The proposition is new, Sir; it is the first time it
was ever heard in this House. I am not prepared, Sir--
this House is not prepared, to receive it. The measure
implies a distrust of His Majesty's government: their
disapproval is sufficient to warrant opposition.
Precaution only is requisite where danger is
apprehended. Here the high character of the in-
dividuals in question is a sufficient guarantee against
any ground for alarm. Give not, then, your sanction to
this measure; for, whatever be its character, if you do
give your sanction to it, the same man by whom this is
proposed, will propose to you others to which it will
be impossible to give your consent. I care very
little, Sir, for the ostensible measure; but what is
there behind it? What are the honourable gentleman's
future schemes? If we pass this bill, what fresh con-
cessions may he not require? What further degradation
is he planning for his country? Talk of evil and
inconvenience, Sir! Look to other countries--study
other aggregations and societies of men, and then see
whether the laws of this country demand a remedy or
deserve a panegyric. Was the honourable gentleman (let
me ask him) always of this way of thinking? Do I not
remember when he was the advocate in this House of very
opposite opinions? I not only quarrel with his present
sentiments, Sir, but I declare very frankly, I do not
like the party with which he acts. If his own motives
were as pure as possible, they cannot but suffer con-
tamination from those with whom he is politically

27

associated. This measure may be a boon to the constitution; but I will accept no favour to the constitution from such hands. [Loud cries of Hear! Hear!] I profess myself, Sir, an honest and upright member of the British Parliament, and I am not afraid to profess myself an enemy to all change and all innovation. I am satisfied with things as they are; and it will be my pride and pleasure to hand down this country to my children as I received it from those who preceded me. The honourable gentleman pretends to justify the severity with which he has attacked the noble Lord who presides in the Court of Chancery; but I say such attacks are pregnant with mischief to Government itself. Oppose Ministers, you oppose Government; disgrace Ministers, you disgrace Government; bring Ministers into contempt, you bring Government into contempt; and anarchy and civil war are the consequences. Besides, Sir, the measure is unnecessary. Nobody complains of disorder in that shape in which it is the aim of your measure to propose a remedy to it. The business is one of the greatest importance; there is need of the greatest caution and circumspection. Do not let us be precipitate, Sir. It is impossible to foresee all consequences. Everything should be gradual: the example of a neighbouring nation should fill us with alarm! The honourable gentleman has taxed me with illiberality, Sir. I deny the charge. I hate innovation, but I love improvement. I am an enemy to the corruption of Government, but I defend its influence. I dread reform, but I dread it only when it is intemperate. I consider the liberty of the Press as the great Palladium of the Constitution; but, at the same time, I hold the licentiousness of the Press in the greatest abhorrence. Nobody is more conscious than I am of the splendid abilities of the honourable mover, but I tell him at once, his scheme is too good to be practicable. It savours of Utopia. It looks well in theory, but it won't do in practice. It will not do, I repeat, Sir, in practice; and so the advocates of the measure will find, if, unfortunately, it should find its way through Parliament. [Cheers] The source of that corruption to which the honourable member alludes, is in the minds of the people: so rank and extensive is that corruption, that no political reform can have any effect in removing it. Instead of reforming others--instead of reforming the State, the Constitution, and every thing that is most excellent, let each man reform himself! Let him look at home; he will find there enough to do, without looking abroad, and aiming at what is out of his power. [Loud cheers]

And now, Sir, as it is frequently the custom in this House to end with a quotation, and as the gentleman who preceded me in the debate has anticipated me in my favourite quotation of 'The strong pull and the long pull,' I shall end with the memorable words of the assembled Barons--'<u>Nolumus leges Angliae mutari</u>' [translated, 'We do not want the laws of England to be changed']."

The Counterplan and the Counterproposal

The third and final strategy available to the negative is the counterplan or the counterproposal. The counterplan is suitable for propositions of policy, whereas the counterproposal is applicable to propositions of fact and value.

When disputing propositions of policy, it is sometimes a necessary strategy for the negative to admit the stock issue of need when, in its opinion, the status quo cannot be defended and a pure refutation would probably not succeed. Having admitted the need, the negative then offers a counterplan, literally a new plan of its own, which it believes will better solve or satisfy the need than the affirmative plan. The negative, just as the affirmative, must also demonstrate that its counterplan will satisfy the admitted need. Thereafter, the need issue <u>per se</u> drops from the debate because the affirmative has won it via the negative's admission. The clash is then over whose plan best solves the need.

When debating a proposition of fact or value, it sometimes behooves the negative to advance a counterproposal. Assume the proposition, "X is guilty of the murder of Y." The negative may decide that there is not enough evidence to defend X, and perhaps a pure refutation is not advisable, either. If, however, the negative believes that substantial evidence exists to argue that Z is guilty of the murder of Y, then the stage is set for a counterproposal strategy. If the defense can prove that Z did it, then clearly X could not have done it. For this strategy, the negative admits the need, in this case a corpse, but argues a counterproposal for its cause. That is, Z had the presence, means, and motive to kill Y. The disputation is then over whether X or Z had the better means, presence, and motive to kill Y.

However, the judging of counterplans or proposals,

and this determines ultimately how one will argue them effectively, can present a problem. To be sure, a verdict for the negative would obtain if the counterplan were clearly superior to the affirmative's plan, or for the affirmative if the defense's counterproposal for Z was weaker than that for X. But what about the not unlikely situation in which the affirmative's and the negative's proofs seem to be at a dead heat? In a debate without the counter strategies, one will remember that a tie would go to the negative because of presumption and of the affirmative's inability to meet the criterion of preponderance of proof on the contested issues. But in a tie situation, with counter strategies, is the judging paradigm different?

In advancing a counterplan or counterproposal, the negative must meet two tests in order to win. Obviously, the affirmative would argue that one or both of these tests were not fulfilled, and hence the negative's counterstrategy should fall. The first test is _mutual exclusivity_. The affirmative's plan and the negative's counter strategy must be mutually exclusive, must mutually exclude one another, and one could not adopt both plans simultaneously, i.e., if there were only one killer, then both X and Z could not be guilty but only one of them would be. The second test is the _competitiveness_ of the counterplan or proposal. The counter strategy must be better, more desirable, more persuasive, than the affirmative's plan. This is because the negative has sacrificed presumption by admitting the need and, assuming the affirmative carries its plan, it has discharged its prima facie case. Since, in effect, the negative becomes another "affirmative," as it were, in the debate round, it should have to prove its counterplan or proposal better just as the affirmative originally had to do via the status quo. Thus, in a tie situation, with a counterplan or counterproposal strategy, the negative would lose.

NOTES

1For a fuller discussion of the classical system of stasis, see Halford Ross Ryan, "_Kategoria_ and _Apologia_: On Their Rhetorical Criticism as a Speech Set," _Quarterly Journal of Speech_, 68 (1982), 254-61.

2John C. Calhoun, "The Slavery Question," in _American Public Addresses, 1740-1952_, ed. A. Craig Baird (New York: McGraw-Hill, 1956), p. 83.

3Wendell Phillips, "Murder of Lovejoy," in *American Public Addresses, 1740-1952*, pp. 139-40.

4Clarence Seward Darrow, "To the Jury: Self-Defense," in *Great American Speeches, 1898-1963*, ed. John Graham (New York: Meredith Corp., 1970), p. 35.

5Huey Pierce Long, "Every Man a King," in *American Rhetoric from Roosevelt to Reagan*, ed. Halford Ross Ryan (Prospect Heights: Waveland Press, 1983), p. 46.

6Abraham Lincoln, "Lincoln-Douglas Joint Debate at Alton," in *American Public Addresses, 1740-1952*, p. 106.

7See Joseph R. McCarthy, "The Red-Tinted Washington Crowd," in Charles Lomas, *The Agitator in American Society* (Englewood Cliffs: Prentice-Hall, Inc., 1968), p. 160; and "Speech to Senate," in *Joseph R. McCarthy*, ed. Allen J. Matusow (Englewood Cliffs: Prentice-Hall, Inc., 1970), p. 26.

8William Lowndes Yancey, "For Southern Rights," *American Public Addresses, 1740-1952*, p. 120.

9Richard Milhous Nixon, "My Side of the Story," *American Rhetoric from Roosevelt to Reagan*, p. 122.

10Robert Thornwell, "The Rights and Duties of Masters," in *Sermons in American History*, ed. Dewitte Holland (Nashville: Abingdon Press, 1971), p. 227.

11See Michael C. Leff, *Rhetorical Timing in Lincoln's "House Divided" Speech* (Evanston: Northwestern Univ., 1984), p. 9.

12See John Calhoun, "The Slavery Question," p. 83.

13See Abraham Lincoln, "Lincoln-Douglas Joint Debate," p. 106.

14John Kennedy, "Opening Statement," *Great American Speeches, 1898-1963*, p. 110.

ADDITIONAL READINGS

Hample, Dale. "Motives in Law: An Adaptation of Legal Realism." *Journal of the American Forensic Association*, 15 (1979), 156-168.

Parkinson, Michael G., Geisler, Deborah, and Pelias, Mary Hinchcliff. "The Effect of Verbal Skills on Trial Successes." *Journal of the American Forensic Association*, 20 (1983), 16-22.

Reinard, John C. and Reynolds, Rodney A. "The Effects of Inadmissible Testimony Objections and Rulings on Jury Decisions." *Journal of the American Forensic Association*, 15 (1978), 91-109.

QUESTIONS FOR REFLECTION

1. What are the negative's options in discharging the burden of rebuttal?

2. What are *argumentum ad vercudiam, misericordiam, populum, hominem, personam, crenam, ignorantium, baculum*?

3. What are *petitio principii, non sequitur, post hoc ergo propter hoc, reductio ad absurdam*?

4. What are turning-the-tables, amphiboly, loaded words, posing a dilemma, straw issues?

5. When are counterplans and counterproposals appropriate to argue?

6. What are the two tests by which one judges and argues counter strategies?

Section Three:
Affirmative and Negative Rebuttals

Now that the debater has a clear understanding of
how, in their respective constructive speeches, the affirmative discharges its burden of proof, and the negative may meet its burden of rebuttal by choosing one or
more of the three strategies, it is time to treat the
rebuttal speech.

The rebuttal speech, for both the affirmative and
negative, has two functions: (1) it must rebuild or
extend its own case, and (2) it must refute the opposing case. Both of these functions blend into the steps
in attack and defense [to be discussed in the next
section] toward the ultimate persuasive proof of how
one's analysis seriously harms the opponent's case or
significantly sustains one's own case.

The focus of the rebuttal speech is on issues.
For the affirmative, it is extending and carrying all
of the issues in the prima facie case. For the
negative, it is refuting and rebuilding the issues of
the negative stance or case. This is not to say that
neither side refutes or extends on evidence and
arguments, but that such a rebuttal has as its ultimate
goal the acceptance or rejection of vital issues.

Given that rebuttal speeches are almost always al-
lotted less time than constructive speeches, the affirmative and negative have to be very selective in the
arguments and evidence they choose to debate versus
what they will quietly and tacitly drop. If the affirmative spoke for 8 minutes, and the negative gave an
8 minute constructive speech, then the affirmative's 4
minute rebuttal must necessarily compress 16 minutes
worth of argument into 4, and, following that, the
negative would have to deal with 20 minutes of argumentation in 4 minutes of its rebuttal. Given the time
constraints, what is the best rebuttal strategy? There
are no easy answers or inflexible rules to follow because a rebuttal strategy is determined by a number of
factors in the debate situation which contribute to so
many combinations that there is not enough time nor
space to account for all of them here. However, some
general guidelines can be gauged.

The affirmative's choices in its rebuttal are
rather more limited than the negative's options because
the affirmative has to extend, and refute where

33

attacked, all of the issues in the prima facie case. So first, the affirmative must extend all of the contested issues, or risk losing only one of them and hence the entire debate. Second, the affirmative has to refute in two general areas: (1) where the negative has made a serious charge or damage to the prima facie case and/or has established a major argument and evidence for its case, that negative analysis must be refuted and destroyed or the negative may carry it, much to the affirmative's consternation; and (2) where the affirmative has a reasonable chance of winning "weaker" negative arguments and evidence, argumentative emphasis should be placed there. In other words, the affirmative eschews in the rebuttal speech disputation on minor negative arguments because the negative could win a few minor battles but not win the war.

The negative choices in its rebuttal are less constricted than the affirmative's because the negative does not have to extend or refute all of the issues, but can, at the very minimum, "drop" all of the issues save one and still win the debate. Usually, however, a wise negative will not place all of its hopes on only one issue. Thus, the negative has the same general approach that the affirmative has, but it is not so tightly constrained in its options. First, the negative will extend the issues in its case (although it could drop one or two weak ones in order to concentrate on winning the stronger ones). Second, the negative would refute where the affirmative had inflicted significant damage and/or where the negative believed it could win relatively "weaker" arguments. It would not want to waste its valuable rebuttal time in extending and/or refuting unimportant evidence or arguments because that tactic may win a few small skirmishes but lose the larger war.

Admittedly, rebuttal speeches are more difficult to deliver than constructive speeches. One has to speak extemporaneously with little foreknowledge of what arguments and evidence one's opponent will choose to extend, refute, or even drop. But the practice of several rounds of debate will enhance the debater's ability to give a good rebuttal. If one has firmly in mind the format and the goals for the affirmative and negative rebuttals, then, with practice, one can trust one's intelligence to apply the substance of the argument to the form.

The Flowsheet. The last skill, but certainly an important one, the debater must master is how to write or
take a flowsheet. A flowsheet is a kind of abbreviated
debate shorthand notation which portrays the flow or
progression of the debate from constructive speeches
through the rebuttals. In lieu of the impracticality
of representing a flowsheet here (your instructor will
show you its format and how it is done), some general
guidelines can be mentioned in order to prepare oneself
for actual instruction in the classroom.

The paper one selects to write on should be at
least 8-1/2 x 14 legal size paper, and turned on its
side in order to flow the arguments lengthwise. Some
student debaters find commercially available artist's
sketch pads to be more convenient to use because of
their larger size. In either case, divide the flow
sheet equally into as many parts as there are constructive and rebuttal speeches. Each speech will be flowed
in its part.

One would also be advised to purchase a commercially available ballpoint pen which has four colors in
it; or failing that, one should have two ballpoint pens
of different and contrasting colors. Thus, one writes
down the affirmative's constructive speech and rebuttal
in one color, and the negative's speeches in another
color. The contrasting colors immediately identify the
different sides and also make it easier to distinguish
at a glance one's case or the opponent's when speaking
from a flowsheet.

QUESTIONS FOR REFLECTION

1. What are the two major functions of a rebuttal?

2. What is the major argumentative focus of a
    rebuttal?

3. Can the affirmative drop issues in a rebuttal?

4. Can the negative drop issues in a rebuttal?

5. What rebuttal options are available to the
    affirmative?

6. What rebuttal options are open to the negative?

35

Section Four: Attack and Defense

The process of attack and defense is how the debater actually argues in the debate situation. The process is used by both the affirmative and negative speakers throughout the debate. The affirmative, in the prima facie case, may use this process to go on the offensive to attack probable negative argumentation and/or to attack probable negative attacks on the prima facie case. As one of the functions of discharging the burden of rebuttal, the negative might employ the process in its first constructive speech. Both sides will use the steps in their rebuttal speeches. The process is the form of the argument, the debater supplies the substance in the formula from the case. A typical analysis for each of the three types of propositions is illustrated in the following three steps in attack and defense:

1. State your objection to the evidence and/or argument you will refute. "The prosecution cannot claim a positive identification of the defendant by M." "The affirmative has used weak evidence to prove that General Lee was the better general." "The negative has not denied that acid rain kills fish and plants."

2. Support your objection with counter evidence and/or argument. "M could not see well because it was dark outside, there was no moon shining, and he was too far away; therefore, M's identification is not positive at all." "Most of the affirmative's sources are biased toward the South, and none of them are expert military historians but rather ordinary veterans." "Remember that the qualified wildlife experts and university scientists which the affirmative quoted still stand unrefuted by the negative."

3. Demonstrate how your proof prevails on a contested issue. "Since the prosecution cannot sustain an identification on M's insufficient testimony, the prosecution fails to establish M's presence and the prima facie case falls." "Therefore, the affirmative cannot prove the prima facie issue of better tactician, and the case collapses because of the affirmative's inability to sustain that issue." "Since the negative has not denied the analysis presented in the constructive speech, and given that the affirmative has extended in

rebuttal that acid rain kills fish and plants, I call for an affirmation from the judge on the issue."

This process of attack and defense is applied over and over, by both the affirmative and the negative speakers, as the debate progresses. Especially in the rebuttals, it is necessary to show how one's evidence and argument are sustaining, or destroying, a contested issue. The affirmative, one will remember, must maintain a preponderance of proof on the contested issues, whereas the negative may concentrate its attack on only one, or more, of the prima facie issues. For either side, the attack and defense process must be used to prevail with the persuasive proof at the conclusion of the debate. The wise debater will memorize the process so that in the heat of the actual debate, the debater can insert the appropriate evidence and argument into the three step formula as second nature. One's ability to argue effectively is contingent upon mastering the steps and applying them in the debate situation.

Section Five: Direct and Cross-Examination

One of the skills which differentiates the debater from the orator is the ability to conduct effective and telling direct and cross-examination of witnesses or of one's opponent. Direct and cross-examination are features of the forensic format which signalize the debater's mastery over the debate situation. Direct examination may be said to occur when the debater questions a witness which is acknowledged to be eager and favorable to the questioner. Cross-examination may be said to occur when the debater queries a witness or opponent acknowledged to be reluctant and unfavorable to the questioner.

Procedure in Direct Examination

1. Of each witness, ask one or two preliminary fielding questions to put the witness at ease, and to establish the name, occupation, and perhaps the relationship to the case.

2. Then proceed to ask questions which will elicit the following kinds of responses:

   a) to establish a unit or chain of evidence.
   b) to support evidence with an argument.
   c) to use evidence to refute counter evidence.
   d) to use an argument to counter an argument.
   e) to pre-empt an attack by the opponent on one's argument or evidence.

It is often useful to allow the witness to tell in a narrative form the evidence and argument, but the direct examiner wisely recapitulates at the conclusion of the time period with direct questions to summarize the salient points made by the respondent. Direct examination should be well planned, the questions should be constructed to evoke the desired answer, and the time limit for questioning used optimally for the most important evidence and argument.

While the debater will naturally tend to look at the witness in direct examination, it is a good idea to keep an eye on the judge's face to see what reactions, if any, are discernible. This is to gauge the relative strengths and weaknesses of the evidence and argument evoked during the period of examination. Eye-contact with the judge, to be discussed more fully in chapter five, is important because it may allow the debater to assess what arguments to stress, and what ones to ignore, in rebuttal speeches as a function of the judge's feedback on the issues during the direct examination period.

Procedure in Cross-Examination

In the cross-examination period, the debater queries a reluctant witness, or an opponent who is obviously reluctant to make harmful admissions. Great care must be taken in cross-examination to insure in the process maximum benefit to oneself and minimum damage to one's case. The end of cross-examination is two-fold: (1) to extract from the opponent favorable admissions for one's own case, and (2) to extract from the opponent harmful admissions for the respondent's case. Throughout the questioning period, the questioner **must always maintain control** over the reluctant witness or opponent. There are several rules to follow in order to maintain control and to elicit the optimal responses:

a) do phrase questions so that you can seek a simple yes or no answer, "Did you see X have the gun?" and press for the yes or no response.

b) do **quickly**, but **politely**, interrupt and cut off a respondent if the respondent is answering too much, "Yes, I did see X with the gun, but she was . . .," "Thank you, very much, let me ask my next question."

c) if it is necessary to ask a chain of questions, seek one link and one answer at a time, "Did you see X have the gun?" "Did X point the gun at Y?" "Did X have a moment or two to reflect before X pulled the trigger?"

d) do not ask complex questions (a wise respondent will answer favorable portions of the complex question and "forget" to answer, hoping you will forget, too, the unfavorable parts).

e) do not ask extended questions (both the judge and the opponent may not know or remember what was sought, and the respondent may rightly make you appear foolish by asking you, "Was that a question or a speech?").

f) do not allow the respondent to answer one's

39

question with a question--whose cross-examination
period is it? (You could restate the question and
request that it be answered, and with recalcitrant
opponents, you could say "I'll be more than happy
to answer your questions in your cross-examination
period.")

g) do not ask questions which invite extended
answers (you will lose control).

h) do not ask and then proceed to answer your own
question (this indicates inept cross-
examination skills and probably indicates your
inability to phrase the appropriate question to
make the opponent answer in the desired
fashion).

The procedure of cross-examination follows the first
step of direct examination, supra. The second step is
different in that it attempts to secure the following
kinds of admissions from the opponent that:

a) one or more of the classifications of evidence
cast doubt on the ground of belief for the
opponent's case or bolster one's case.

b) one or more of the tests of evidence damage the
credibility of the proof for the opponent's
case or strengthen one's case.

c) the evidence or argument does not support the
opponent's analysis or it does support one's
reasoning.

d) inconsistencies, internally or externally,
exist in the opponents case and not in one's
case.

Since debate is an academic activity consistent with
the search for truth or the apparent truth, it is ethically important for the viability of cross-examination
that the respondent answer questions truthfully and
forthrightly; however, that does not mean that the
respondent is logically or ethically obligated to
answer more than is asked. The debater may find the
testimony for practice direct and cross-examination of
witnesses in Part II to be helpful in analyzing the
desired responses and in honing the examination skills
in practice situations.

CHAPTER FIVE

DELIVERY IN DEBATE

Persuasive advocacy depends in a large measure on the debater's delivery skills. Many writers, for instance, have complained that some debaters often talk too fast,[1] and to a degree these critics are correct. Because debaters generally speak under time restraints, which the orator usually does not observe, there is a natural tendency to cram as much verbiage into a speech as one can, yet that is not necessarily good debating technique.[2] An effective debating form in terms of delivery can be delineated in terms of the debater's voice management, gestures, and eye-contact.

<u>Voice Management</u>. The debater can manipulate three voice variables in order to enhance the persuasibility of the voice. First, the debater can vary the rate of speaking. As a rule, most debaters do speak at a rate faster than ordinary talk, but the debate rate should not appreciably exceed a conversational mode of address. The debater should communicate at a speaking rate that is comprehensible and comfortable for the judge to listen to. Live audiences and judges do not tolerate garbled and unintelligibly fast speech.[3] Important evidence and arguments can be orally emphasized by slowing down to let the judge digest their impact. Less important language can be hurried along a bit in compensation for that elongation of salient points. Second, the debater can vary the pitch of the voice. The speaker can raise or lower the pitch, in its musical sense, to emphasize points, to draw attention to important tests of evidence, etc. One should eschew the sing-song pitch patterns of some debaters who figuratively "sing" the same pitch patterns no matter what the sense or meaning of the language is. Third, the debater can vary the loudness or volume of the voice. Again, the normal volume of loudness which one uses in everyday conversation is an appropriate benchmark for debating. However, changes in the loudness, either increasing or decreasing the volume, can emphasize salient points.

The debater needs to manage the voice with an eye toward variety and emphasis. The rate, loudness, and pitch can be employed independently or in some agreeable combination in order to express the whole range of human expression. This will enable the debater to be a

41

persuasive communicator. The debater's aim is to persuade, not to overpower, or dramatize, or harangue, the judge. Attractiveness in delivery is just as important to the debater as it is to the orator.

Gestures. Orators have long known that gestures make the address more persuasive, and gestures similarly make the debater more credible. Facial gestures--the askance look for a piece of weak evidence, the roll of the eyes to indicate astonishment at a spurious argument, the shake of the head to stress and bolster assent or negation in the langauge; hand and arm gestures--to support visually an argument with the upturned palm, or to reject an argument with the "throwaway" gesture; and the entire body--leaning forward to impress a point on the judge, or leaning backward in order to signal "that evidence does not say what my opponent says it does," all of these gestures, and many others like them, reinforce and emphasize the language of the case. Debate is a kind of oral duel, and the wise debater would utilize both language and gestures to prevail persuasively over the opponent.

Eye-contact. The establishment of direct eye-contact with the judge is just as important to the debater as it is to the orator. If all other factors are held constant, the more eye-contact a speaker exhibits to the listener, the more credible is that speaker. Debaters also need to be sensitive to the body-language feedback from the judge. If the debater is looking at the judge, the debater can perceive that the judge's questioning look may mean that the argument is unclear, then it should be reiterated by bringing clarifying language and arguments to bear; a subtle nod in agreement may indicate that the debater should stress that argument because the speaker is probably winning it; or boredom and inattention may indicate a need for the debater to slow down, to vary the pitch or loudness, etc., in order to re-establish the judge's attention to the debate. But these, and other such forms of valuable feedback, cannot be perceived if the debater is not establishing direct eye-contact with the judge. Because debaters often must speak from a flow-sheet, they will by that fact tend to have less eye-contact than the orator. But effective eye-contact can never be accomplished by focusing one's head and eyes on the flow-sheet. The debater should practice especially the constructive speech enough times so that it can be delivered in a manner approximating an address. The rebuttal, because of a necessary reliance on the flow-sheet for the extensions of the arguments, will probably have less eye-contact than the constructive speech; nevertheless, an appropriate amount of eye-contact is requisite in the rebuttal, too.

In fine, the delivery techniques of the orator apply as well to the debater in the debate situation. It is the naive debater who imagines otherwise.

NOTES

1See Henry McGuckin, "Better Forensics: An Impossible Dream?" Journal of the American Forensic Association, 8 (1972), 182-85.

2Janet M. Vasilius and Dan DeStephen, "An Investigation of the Relationship Between Debate Tournament Success and Rate, Evidence, and Jargon," Journal of the American Forensic Association, 15 (1979), 203.

3See Kurt Ritter, "Recapturing the Rhetorical Dimension: Debating in Campus Forums," Speaker and Gavel, 12 (1974), 1-3, and John K. Boaz, "A Footnote to William Southworth's Critique of the Final Round of the 1984 National Debate Tournament," Journal of the American Forensic Association, 21 (1984), 119-22.

QUESTIONS FOR REFLECTION

1. What are the three voice variables?

2. What are the ends of vocal management?

3. What are the three major kinds of gestures?

4. Why is eye-contact important?

PART II

CASES FOR ARGUMENTATION AND DEBATE

THE JOHNSON CASE

Is Mr. Johnson guilty of dangerous driving?

Among the various sections defining dangerous driving in the township of Watering Springs are the following pertinent ones:

Section II, Paragraph B: All operators of motor driven vehicles must signal, via hand or electric device, their intention to turn at least fifty feet before the intersection.

Section II, Paragraph F: All operators of motor driven vehicles must have their vehicles under control at all times while on the highway. An operator who collides with the rear of another vehicle is in violation.

Section IX, Paragraph A: All drivers should exercise reasonable care in operating their vehicles. All drivers are enjoined to avoid accident-inducing situations whenever possible.

On August 17, Officer Hadley cited Mr. Alvin Johnson to appear in Watering Springs Court to answer charges of violating Section II, Paragraph B and Section IX, Paragraph A. Officer Hadley filed the following report and attached sketch.

HOMER GEPHARDT, 58 years old, was mowing his lawn when he looked up to see his neighbor, Al Johnson, slowing down to turn into his driveway. At that time, he did not notice the motorcycle. He went back to his mowing when about a few seconds later, he heard a loud "thud" sound. He looked at the street to see a motorcycle overturned, and the driver was thrown off about three feet, and Al was just stopping his car about fifteen feet in front of his driveway. He did not see the actual accident. He went into his house and called the police, and about seven minutes later Officer Hadley arrived.

ALVIN JOHNSON. I was returning home from the supermarket. As I approached my home, I turned on the turn signal--I always turn it on when I reach my neighbor's driveway as it gives adequate time before I actually turn in. When I was about twenty or thirty feet from my driveway, I looked into the rearview mirror and I noticed this motorcycle, about ten or fifteen feet behind me. He appeared to be slowing for my turn. When I was about ten feet from my driveway, I was suddenly hit from the rear by the motorcycle. I pulled my car off the road and stayed in my car until the police arrived. I was very nervous and shaken somewhat. I remember that the motorcycle, the one and only time I saw it behind me before it hit me, seemed to be in the left hand part of the right lane. I did not think anything of it because these fool kids are often all over the road.

LARRY ADAMS. I was riding my motorcycle behind this car (identified as Mr. Johnson's) and I noticed that he had his right turn signal on. A second or so later, his brake lights went on, so I was sure he was going to make a right hand turn onto Maple Street. I started to pass him on the left when suddenly the idiot made a left turn. As I was almost passing him, I could not avoid keeping my cycle from ramming into his left rear bumper. I did not remember anything after that until I woke up in the hospital. Under no circumstances was I exceeding the speed limit of 25 mph.

OFFICER HADLEY responded to the station call and was on the scene at 2:37 pm. He ascertained that Mr. Johnson, although a bit shaken and nervous, was unhurt from the accident. The motorcyclist, Larry Adams, was still lying in the street with a severely injured leg (at the hospital it was determined to be broken) so he called an ambulance which arrived about ten minutes later. Because of the intense pain of the victim, no questions were attempted at the scene. He did, however, attempt to question Mr. Johnson. He measured a single skid mark, obviously that of the motorcycle, which stretched for about ten feet and then it stopped. The front of the motorcycle was damaged, the front tire burst, and the tire rim substantially bent. There were no automobile tire tracks at the scene. He questioned Mr. Gephardt, but there were no other witnesses to the accident.

ROSCOE HARDING, insurance investigator, submitted that total damages to Adam's motorcycle were $357.55 and damage to Johnson's rear bumper assembly was $147.85.

ADMITTED FACTS.   Mr. Adams, aged 17, was in a pilot
program for insuring motorcyclists under a two-thirds
rate reduction.   If he were found guilty of dangerous
driving, his two speeding tickets--one for 29 mph in a
25 mph zone and the second one for 64 mph in a 55 zone
--would remove him from the program.   His father stated
that he would have to pay the full rates himself.
Since Adams has not graduated from high school and is
unemployed, he cannot pay the full rates and would effectively loose his motorcycle.   Mr. Johnson, aged 73,
if convicted, would have to attend "Safe Driving
School" every six months in order to get his license
renewed on a semi-annual basis.

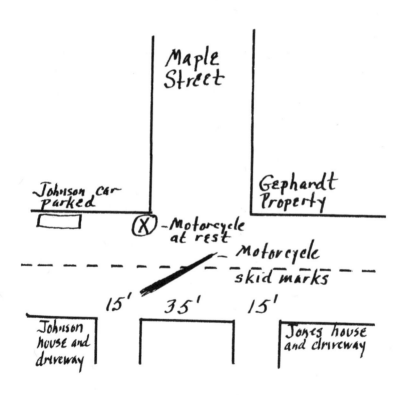

THE JOHNSON CASE: A SAMPLE BRIEF FOR THE PROSECUTION

Proposition: "Mr. Johnson is guilty of dangerous driving."

Introduction

I. This case is important because

    A. Dangerous driving is against the law, and

    B. The motorcyclist, Larry Adams, was severely injured.

II. The facts on which all parties agree are

    A. The following map, attached, by Officer Hadley, and

    B. The front tire and rim of the motorcycle was damaged severely, and

    C. There were motorcycle skid marks of about 10', and

    D. Larry Adams has two speeding tickets: 28/25, and 62/55.

III. Definitions of terms are

    A. "reasonable care": "That degree of care which a person of ordinary prudence would exercise in the same or similar circumstances" (Black's Law Dictionary, p. 1138), and

    B. "accident-inducing situations": "contemplates any situation occurring on the highway wherein he so operates his automobile as to cause injury to the property or person of another using the same highway" (Ibid., p. 14).

IV. The issues are as follows

    A. Section II, Par. B: Did Mr. Johnson signal 50' before an intersection?, and

    B. Section IX, Par. A: Did Mr. Johnson exercise

reasonable care in avoiding an accident inducing situation?

V. Waived issues

    A.   None.

Proof

I.   Mr. Johnson did not signal 50' before the intersection [Section II, Par. B], for

    A.   There is no testimony which states he sig-
naled LEFT, and

    B.   Motorcyclist Larry Adams states it was a
RIGHT signal, and

        1.   Larry Adams' veracity is not in dispute,
and

    C.   "At least 50' before an intersection" is in
doubt, and

        1.   turning on at neighbor's driveway is not
enough, and

        2.   margin of error could be present in
faulty memory.

    D.   Therefore, Mr. Johnson most likely gave a
RIGHT signal less than 50' from the
intersection.

II.   Mr. Johnson did not exercise "reasonable care" in
"accident-inducing situations," for

    A.   There was no reasonable care, nor ordinary
prudence, and

        1.   he admits he only looked once, and

        2.   this is not what a prudent person would
do, and

    B.   Mr. Johnson did not avoid an accident induc-
ing situation, and

        1.   he injured Larry Adams severely, and

2. he did not contemplate a situation, and

    a. he admits the motorcycle appeared in the left part of the lane, and

    b. this action is not what a prudent person would do, and

C. Mr. Johnson was not motivated to exercise reasonable care, and

    1. he testifies: "These fool kids are often all over the road," and

    2. this foreknowledge should have compelled him to exercise more reasonable care.

D. Therefore, Mr. Johnson did not exercise reasonable care in accident inducing situations.

Conclusion

Since

I. Mr. Johnson did not signal 50' before an intersection, and as

II. Mr. Johnson did not exercise reasonable care in accident-inducing situations,

Therefore,

"Mr. Johnson is guilty of dangerous driving."

Note:

1. The brief is divided into three sections: Introduction, Proof, and Conclusion.

2. The language of the brief is logical and straightforward.

3. Use topical outlining with fairly complete sentences.

4. Each subpoint must explain or illustrate its superior point, it answers the question, "Why?"

5. The brief may be typed or written, but in either case it must be <u>double-spaced</u> throughout.

THE JOHNSON CASE: A SAMPLE AFFIRMATIVE SPEECH OUTLINE

Introduction.

Because dangerous driving is against the law, and because Mr. Larry Adams has been badly injured, the prosecution will prove that Mr. Johnson is guilty of dangerous driving.

Discussion.

I. First, I contend that Johnson did not signal correctly. Section II, Paragraph B: "All operators of motor driven vehicles must signal, via hand or electric devices, their intention to turn at least (50') before the intersection."

   A. Mr. Johnson does not say he signaled left.

   B. Motorcyclist Adams says it was a right signal.

   C. At neighbor's driveway, only a bare 50'

      1. under these circumstances, should signal more than 50'.

   D. In sum, it is most likely that a right signal was made and the 50' distance is in serious doubt.

II. Second, I shall prove that Johnson did not exercise "reasonable care" to avoid an accident.

   Section IX, Paragraph A: "All drivers should exercise reasonable care in operating their vehicles. All drivers are enjoined to avoid accident-inducing situations whenever possible." By defining reasonable care as "logical caution," we can see that Johnson could have avoided this accident.

   A. By his own admission, Johnson admits he only looked once--is this logical caution?

51

B.   By his own admission, the motorcycle ap-
     peared in the left part of the lane--
     should not Johnson have exercised more
     caution?

C.   Johnson is not motivated to exercise
     logical caution because he does not like
     "fool kids" who are all over the road--
     but where is Johnson's caution?

D.   So, by his own admission, Johnson did
     not exercise reasonable care.

III. Third, and last, the prosecution will prove
     that there were mitigating circumstances in
     regard to rear-end collision.

A.   Johnson had on a right signal, so it was
     only reasonable for Adams to pass, but
     Johnson turned left--What could Adams do
     but hit him?

B.   The tire skid marks make it almost im-
     possible for Johnson to pull into his
     driveway as he stated.

     1.   Johnson parked his car on the
          right, thus confirming the
          contention.

Conclusion.

To summarize this case, the prosecution has proven
(1) that Johnson did not give a correct signal; (2)
that he did not use reasonable care; and (3) that there
were mitigating circumstances for the rear-end
collision. We have proved the case beyond a reasonable
doubt, and therefore call for a verdict of guilty as
charged.

THE ASH CASE

Is Vernon Ash guilty of smoking marijuana?

Section 97 of the State Institutes of Laws reads:
    The smoking of, the use of, the possession of
    marijuana is a felony. Upon conviction of this
    felony, the automatic sentence is five years in
    the State Penitentiary with no parole.

On Saturday night, September 15, Detective Lieutenant
Harris, along with three other members of the State
Narcotics Division, raided an apartment which was
rented to John Colby, a junior at State University.
Harris arrested Colby along with Harry Keel (a senior
at State University), Linda Morely (a junior at State
University), and Margie Davis (a senior at State
University). Also arrested was Vernon Ash, a junior at
State University. Colby, Keel, Morely, and Davis all
pleaded guilty to the smoking of marijuana. Ash
pleaded not guilty and was tried separately.

DETECTIVE LIEUTENANT HARRIS. Our Division had been
operating for about two months on the campus of State
University. We received an anonymous telephone call
that Colby was holding another one of his "pot
parties." We obtained a search warrant, broke down the
door when it was not opened on our command. Upon
entering, Colby and Morely were trying to open a window
which was evidently stuck in place to either escape or
throw out their marijuana cigarettes. At any rate, I
personally arrested Colby and Morely with half-smoked
cigarettes on their person.

OFFICER JOHN MEER. I was attached to Lieutenant
Harris' Division. Upon entering the Colby apartment,
Harris went over to arrest the two at the window
(identified as Colby and Morely). I immediately headed
for two others who were on the floor. I might add that
they would not be presentable on the public streets. I
asked them to get up to get dressed. They had a common
ash tray which I impounded. I administered a breath
test to them immediately after they had dressed. The
results were .35 on the scale and, of course, a reading
of .19 is admissible evidence of smoking marijuana.
The Division Laboratory later informed me that the impounded ash tray had the remains of six marijuana
cigarettes in it, and three of them had lipstick traces

53

which matched those of Davis.

OFFICER PAUL GARVEY. Confirms the story of Harris and Meer. I went on in the apartment as Harris and Meer had things under control in the living room. I searched the bedroom, and seeing no one in there, I tried to go into the bathroom. I heard the toilet flush just before I could open the door. The door was not locked nor did Ash offer any resistance. I made him take the breath test and he registered .21 on the scale. On the basis of this test, I arrested him for the smoking of marijuana.
Cross Examination: Admitted that he did not find any cigarettes on Ash's person, but that Ash had time to flush them down the toilet by the time he opened the door. Admitted that Ash said he had not smoked during the entire evening. Admitted that the only evidence upon which he arrested Ash was a reading of .21 on the breath scale.
Recall, Direct Examination: Has had experience in administering breath tests for the last three years in over seven cases. His ability has never before been questioned.

OFFICER GEORGE NEIL. Was never in the apartment during the actual raid. I was stationed outside the apartment to cover any attempted escapes from within. No one tried to escape from my position at the back of the apartment. After the raid, Harris came to a window to ask me to come in to assist in post-arrest procedures.
Cross Examination: Admitted that he had been at the back of the apartment over looking the bathroom and kitchen windows. Admitted that nothing was discarded from these windows at any time.

KEEL and DAVIS. Testified that they had been involved during most of the evening and had not paid any attention to what Ash was doing. Denied giving Ash any marijuana cigarettes to smoke as they needed them for themselves. Keel was Colby's roommate and had brought Davis to his apartment around 6:30 pm. The Division raided their apartment around 9:30 pm. Not exactly sure when Ash arrived, but estimate it was about eight o'clock or so.

COLBY and MORELY. They had been smoking together since about 6:30 pm on Saturday night. Keel and Davis came in later that night. Not sure when Ash arrived, but had to be before eight o'clock. Ash had come over to Colby and Keel's apartment because the two knew Ash from their sociology class and they had given him an open invitation to come on over to their place sometime.

VERNON ASH. A psychology major in his junior year at State University. He had nothing to do that Saturday night, so he went over to Colby's apartment. He didn't remember exactly, but thought he got there around eight o'clock. Colby answered the door and invited him in, told him to amuse himself, as he (Colby) had his girl with him and would be occupied for the evening. He copied some of Colby's sociology notes in the bedroom for awhile, and came back to the living room, where by this time Keel and Davis were pretty far along. He sat around in the living room for a period of time, and then went to the bathroom to relieve himself, as he was intending to go back to his fraternity house. He was about to flush the toilet when he heard this racket and a loud crash. He flushed the toilet, and was just drying his hands when the policeman entered the bathroom. I submitted without resistance and took the breath test. Contended that he had not smoked at all during the entire time he had been at Colby's party, in fact he had never smoked marijuana before in his life. Cross Examination: Although he admitted that the breath test registered .21 on the scale, he steadfastly maintained that anyone who had been at Colby's party would have had that much in their lungs just from normal respiration. Yes, he knew that smoking marijuana was punishable by a five year prison term, but saw nothing wrong in visiting Colby and staying there after it was obviously apparent that everyone else was smoking.

REVEREND MORRISON. I was astonished when I learned of Vernon's arrest. He attended church fairly regularly, seemed a pleasant and dependable student. I could not imagine his smoking marijuana. I had cautioned him to stay away from that Colby and his crowd, as association with him would come to no good. I wish he had followed my good advice.

PROFESSOR LONG. I teach a seminar class in which Colby and Ash, along with three others, are classmates. Colby and Ash seemed fairly friendly, but no more so than other members of the class. Colby always had more liberal ideas when we had class discussions on sociology topics, Ash always seemed more reserved in his opinions, at least when one could get an opinion from him. Ash was a good student and I could vouch for his character.

THE BUSBY CASE

Is Horatio Busby guilty of the first degree murder of
Thelma Busby?

This strange case arose in the District Court of the
Kansas Territory, 1855. Due to the difficult times of
living on the frontier, a "shoot your wife" law was unfortunately enacted into territorial law. As a consequence of this case, the law was eventually repealed
due to citizen outrage. The law was originally passed
to protect the sanctity of the marriage bed, but the
prosecuting attorney thought otherwise in Busby's case.
The following information and points of law are
relevant.

Section IX, Article 5: "First degree murder is the
taking of another human being's life with malice
aforethought. Upon conviction of this heinous crime,
the punishment is hanging by the neck until dead."

Section XII, Article 1: "When, upon discovering a wife
in flagrante delicto, said wife committing adultery,
and without previous malice, the husband may shoot, and
kill if such ensues, said wife."

Section XII, Article 2: "This section is intended to
sanction the importance of the home with husband and
wife in union. Nothing in this section should be construed to condone the willful killing of another
person."

HAROLD and MARY WORK testified that they were next-door
neighbors of the Busby family. They both heard a gunshot from Busby's house. They ran over, the door was
open, and went into the bedroom on the second floor.
Horatio had a rifle in his hand, Thelma Busby was on
the bed, she looked dead, and so did Jack Collins.
Busby said he found them in bed making love and he shot
them both, but only meant to shoot his wife. They both
ran to fetch the doctor. They were very sorry this
happened to their next door neighbors.

MARY WORTH, spinster schoolteacher, heard the gun shot
from Busby's house and ran over to her neighbor's
house. As she was ascending the stairs, Harold and
Mary were coming down to alert the doctor. She noticed
that Mr. Collins was lying on his back beside Mrs.

Busby who was lying on her back in the bed. A sheet
was pulled over Thelma to hide her body. Jack was
without a shirt, and blood was dripping out of his
chest below the arm pit. They both looked dead to me.

REV. HARTUP testified that Thelma had a loose reputation in town. Many of the ladies in the church circle
had told him of her wanton ways. Thelma Busby was not
allowed to step foot in his church, nor in many of the
more respectable homes in town. The Sunday after this
mishap, he preached a sermon on "The Wages of Sin is
Death" which was well received in his church. In his
opinion, Horatio Busby was justified in shooting his
wife to maintain the sacredness of holy marital vows.

JACK COLLINS testified that he had arrived in Red Oak
only three months ago. He had taken a room at
Brookner's Boarding House as he was single. He had met
Thelma at the Brookner's restaurant where she was an
occasional waitress. She was often lonely because her
husband was out on the range for long periods of time.
It is true that he was in bed with Thelma on the day
she was killed. Steadfastly maintained that he had
never committed adultery with her, and did not on the
day in question. Admitted that Thelma was without
clothes, but noted that he had only removed his shirt.
He only remembers her husband coming into the room and
shooting them. He was unconscious after that.

HORATIO BUSBY testified that he arrived home in the
early afternoon because he was not expected before
dusk. He saw a stranger's horse outside the house. He
went inside, heard disgusting moans from upstairs,
broke into his bedroom, saw those two making love, and,
almost without thinking, leveled his rifle at the two
and pulled the trigger. He only meant to shoot his
wife, but doesn't mind that the bullet plugged her
lover, too. His wife was nude in the bed, and he
covered her with a sheet to be more modest. He hopes
this will be a lesson to other wayward women in the
territory that adultery will not be tolerated.

DR. HORACE BROWN was summoned to the Busby home by the
Work's. He examined Thelma Busby and pronounced her
dead. There was a single bullet hole which pierced her
chest right over the heart. He thinks she probably
died instantly. He examined Collins next. He was
having difficulty breathing but was alive. He administered some medical restoratives to Collins and is
thankful that he pulled through. Collins had a bullet

hole which entered his body just below the armpit and the bullet exited two inches below his right nipple. He was fortunate because the bullet did not hit any ribs. That is the reason the bullet went through Collins into Mrs. Busby. Busby told him his wife was having intercourse with him. He attempted to examine Thelma, and to the best of his knowledge and belief, he could find no evidence of sexual intercourse. Brown also admitted that he could not say that they didn't have intercourse.

MARTHA BOWEN, waitress at the Broad Bull Saloon and Restaurant, said that Jack Collins sometimes ate in the establishment. Collins was a fine man from Jolin, Missouri, who had moved farther west to find his fortune. He was not like the other rowdy customers, and was not a womanizer. Jack was a likeable man who treated others with sympathy and understanding.

DR. WAYLAND CORTLAND, a prominent physician from Kansas City, testified that he took two models of Collins' and Thelma Busby's height and weight, and ran an experiment. He found that by comparing the bullet holes in Collins and Thelma, there was little likelihood that they could have possibly have been engaging in adultery. After talking with various people in Red Oak, he concluded that Busby purposefully shot his wife.

HARRY MIDDLETON had told Busby about his wife's rumored goings-on with other men, because none of the other men with whom they worked dare tell Busby because of his mean and jealous temperament toward any mention of his wife. Busby was 49 years old, Thelma was 36, and Jack was 35 years old. From things his wife had told him, he had no doubt at all that Thelma was stepping out on her husband.

REV. JOSIAH WENTWORTH testified that Thelma had sought religious counsel with him on how to deal with her husband's jealous nature. He did not learn any specifics because Busby learned of her visits and forbade Thelma ever to see him again. In his opinion, Hartup could give little meaningful Christian advice to Thelma.

Several character witnesses were called for Collins: he was a gentle man, did not attend church, but was better than many folks who do. Could not imagine his committing adultery. Several witnesses testified that it was

a well-known fact that Thelma slept with men while
Horatio was away. The prosecution objected to hearsay
evidence, but the judge allowed the testimony but cautioned the jury to weigh it carefully in their
deliberations. In his closing speech, the defense
reminded the jury that "not one person has stepped forward or been named as a partner in Thelma's alleged
'generosities.'"

THE HARRINGTON CASE

Is John Harrington guilty of the first degree murder of Jim Bledsoe?

The deceased and his wife of three years, Mary, lived in a three story, three family dwelling on the East End of New York City. On April 11, Bledsoe was shot to death by three bullets from the gun of John Harrington. Only at the insistence of a local citizen's group for law and order was the Prosecuting Attorney forced to try the case.

MARY BLEDSOE. Had been married to Jim Bledsoe for three years. Like most newly married couples, they had had their ups and downs. She often yelled and quarreled with her husband, but they eventually made up. On the evening in question, she and her husband were having a fierce altercation over buying too many dresses. There was considerable yelling. Jim finally left the house, saying that he was finished with her. She ran after him, yelling back at him. When they got out to the street, Jim got into the glove compartment of their car and got a revolver he kept there, and began to wave it around, and suddenly he was shot.

CORA BROWN. A widow, she lives next door adjoining the Bledsoe apartment. On the night in question, she heard loud shouts and looked out her window in time to see Jim get in the car and emerge with a gun. He was shouting something--the distance precluded her hearing exactly what--when suddenly she heard a gunshot, and then some more, and Jim fell on the sidewalk. She had never witnessed any shootings before this one, and she never wants to again.

NICK JOHNSON. Aged fourteen, he was on his evening paper route when he heard the Bledsoe's in another one of their arguments. He was just next door, when he saw Mr. Bledsoe run out of the house and to his car. Mr. Bledsoe emerged from the car with a gun and was waving it around. He was cursing quite a bit, but I remember his saying to Mrs. Bledsoe on the porch: "If you come any closer to me, I'll blow your g--d--- brains out." Almost immediately afterward, he heard gunshots and Mr. Bledsoe was apparently dead.

JOHN HARRINGTON. Father of Mary Bledsoe, he lives in

the first floor apartment of the building he owns. He rents out the second floor to his daughter until they could save to buy a house of their own. He heard loud arguments upstairs, and soon Jim came stomping down the stairs, yelling at Mary, with her coming right after him, yelling back. Jim was uttering threats to Mary about how he was sick and tired of her buying expensive dresses they couldn't afford and how this time, he was leaving her for good. They were both worked up. I went to the door and saw him run to the car. I was scared something would happen, so I ran to get my service revolver which I keep in the kitchen drawer. When I got back, he was aiming his gun at Mary, saying he was going to kill her, and I shot him three times. I would not have a daughter alive if I did not shoot him.

CAPTAIN CONKLING, N.Y.C.P.D., was called to the scene of the accident by Officer Blitzen. The deceased had three gun shot wounds in him, two in the chest and one in the upper abdomen, he was apparently killed instantly. Harrington, whom he knew from twenty-seven years on the force, fifteen of which he and Harrington had worked out of Criminal Division, told him that Bledsoe threatened his daughter's life, and when Bledsoe leveled his gun at Mary, Harrington had to shoot him. Conkling cited Section IX, Article 87 as basis for his decision not to arrest Harrington for murder.

JAMES and MARTHA ADAMS. Tenants in Harrington's third floor apartment, heard the Bledsoe's fighting again. There was a lot of shouting. They were running down the stairs, past the second floor, when Harrington ran into his ground floor apartment. We just got outside the building when Harrington came out with his gun and we just stood there, shocked, as he opened fire on Bledsoe who was standing by his car on the street. They were somewhat shaken by the rush of events, but they remember Harrington muttering to himself on the porch that he knew what to do with that idiot his daughter married.

WES ADKINS. He had gone with Mary Harrington before she was married to Jim. He had quit dating her because he got Mary back from a date two hours late and her old man--Harrington--yelled at him and forcibly shoved him out the door--he tore his suit on the door as he was pushed--and told him that if punks like him couldn't get his daughter back in time, to stop dating her, or else Adkins would find himself in trouble with the police.

FATHER WOLLENSAK. Had often counseled Jim and Mary.
It was his belief that if they could have found an
apartment somewhere else, many of their marital
problems would have been alleviated. He did not know
that Jim kept a pistol, but was sure that such a kind
hearted person could not have meant to shoot his wife.
Harrington stopped coming to church three years ago
when his wife died. From what his friends told me, he
certainly could have benefited from some heavenly grace
and he wouldn't be in the trouble he is now.

OFFICER BLITZEN. Aged twenty-three, has worked for the
NYCPD for two years. Was the second to the top in his
class at the Police Academy. The three bullets which
were extracted from Bledsoe's body were confirmed by
ballistics experts to have come from Harrington's
police special revolver which he is allowed to keep as
a retired police officer from the force. He inter-
viewed the Adams' at the time, and he wrote in his
notebook that James Adams remembered that Harrington
said, "I've got him this time. That little punk has
yelled at my little girl for the last time." He cannot
understand why the Adams have changed their testimony.
He is tired of these older cops using the law for their
own ends, and he therefore urged a citizens force which
is encouraging law and order to re-open the case based
on the evidence he collected. Under cross-examination,
he admitted that Captain Conklin had passed over him to
give a merit raise to another officer, but that
Conkling's message was to let well enough alone.

DR. BLACK. Court appointed psychiatrist, examined Harrington with these results. For age sixty-three, of
reasonable good health. Harrington seems to be emo-
tionally hyper over his daughter, probably as a result
of his losing his wife due to cancer just after his
daughter's marriage. This overpossessiveness is not
uncommon among such patients, but Harrington evidently
had not developed coping mechanisms to deal with the
problem. While Harrington was undoubtedly under emotional stress, he was sane at the time of the shooting.

Harrington's police file was subpoenaed and it contained the following information: his arrest record was
12% better than average, but his conviction record was
23% better than average; his success on the force was
due to perceptions by his superiors, some of which are
recorded here: "Harrington is able to go beyond the

letter of the law to its sprit in getting bystanders to testify for the Prosecution," "I have had a private discussion with Harrington to tell him the force appreciates his ability to investigate crimes, but that his temper with suspects had better be held in check with these new citizen watchdog committees--a good cop like him could get nailed someday."

Section IX, Article 87 states: "When a felony is in progress, with the use of a firearm, anyone may take reasonable actions to prevent such felony from occurring."

THE JONES CASE

Is Charles Jones guilty of the first degree murder of John Vance?

JOHN DALT. I own Dalt's Hardware Store. I know both the defendant and the deceased. About two years ago, I sold the defendant the Bowie knife (identified by Dalt as Prosecution Exhibit A). Jones often hunted and he needed the knife in the forest for skinning, etc. I never knew any hard feelings to exist between Jones and the deceased.

CHARLES "Chuck" BIGGS. I am the owner and bartender of Chuck's Place. I run a clean establishment and have never had any trouble with the cops. I know when a man has reached his limit, and I throw him out. Friday night was a busy night. A lot of customers were in and out. I was busy and could not pay attention to every little thing that happened.
Cross-Examination: I really cannot remember if both Jones and Vance were in my place together. Like I said, it was a busy night. Admitted to running Friday night poker games in the back room, but the games are always quiet, and were only busted twice by the police.

GLADYS POWELL. My job is waitress at Chuck's Place. Friday night was very busy, but I distinctly remember Jones--after three beers, he gave me a dollar tip. He must have been looped, because no one else ever gave me a dollar tip, fifty cents is the best I ever did.
Cross-Examination: Q. You believe Jones was "looped"--to use your expression--only because he gave you a dollar tip? Is that correct? A. Well, a dollar is a big tip. Q. The tip was your only basis for your conclusion, wasn't it? A. Three beers would put most men out, believe me. Q. No further questions, Your Honor.

DEPUTY HARLOW. I have worked under Sheriff Clayton for five years. We have a good working relationship. Vance and Jones often hunted together, they were known for their hunting skills. Jones could throw a Bowie knife into a tree from twenty feet with deadly accuracy; in fact, he once downed a small doe that way. Never knew either the defendant or the deceased to be in any arguments or disagreements.

J. BROWN and M. BOND. Both had been in a hunting party

with Jones and Vance on Friday afternoon. We heard two gun shots--very close to one another--and ran over to where they came from. By that time, Vance and Jones were into one of their usual arguments. This time, Vance was yelling that he had stalked the bear and it was therefore his. Jones contended that he shot first, so the bear was his. We got them quieted down. Vance took the bear.

ARTHUR BLOSSER. County Coroner, Cambres County, for twenty-five years. I was called to the scene of the murder. Vance's body was located about thirty feet from the back door of Chuck's Place, in among some trash barrels in the alley. There had apparently been a struggle for the trash barrels were disarrayed. Death was almost instantaneous from a severe knife wound in the right ventricle. I arrived at the scene of the murder about 12:30 am. Judging from the fact that rigor mortis had not set in and that the body temperature was still 72 degrees, I would estimate that Vance was killed around 10:00-10:45 pm Friday evening.

ORSON HUGHES. Employed the three-to-eleven shift, and was walking home part of the route behind Chuck's Place. I noticed the trash barrels scattered about, went over and investigated, and saw a body. I immediately went in the tavern and called the County Sheriff's Office. I called about at 11:30 pm.

SEYMOUR C. CLAYTON. I am Sheriff of Cambres County and have been for the last seven years. I arrived on the scene of the murder at 11:50. By that time, a crowd had gathered and Deputy Harlow and I had to clear them away before we could begin our investigation. Harlow called the County Coroner at about 12:00. I looked at the corpse and saw the stab wound--right over the heart it was. I know stab wounds when I see them. The knife was two feet from Vance's body. It was that Bowie knife (identified as Pros. Exhibit A). I picked it up and gave it to Harlow to run fingerprint tests. I knew both the defendant and deceased. They weren't your regular Sunday-School types. I asked around the people in Chuck's Place, and the general consensus was that Vance and Jones had been drinking at a poker game in the back room. I went over to Jones' house at 1:45 pm and arrested him when he was unable to account for himself on Friday night.

JAMES SUMNER. Laboratory technician, Center City. Blood stains on the Bowie knife (Pros. Exhibit A)

matched samples taken from the deceased. Ran fingerprint test. The results were that there were
several unidentifiable prints on the knife, but Jones
prints were found around the handle of the knife.

M. BOND (recalled). I know the sound of Jones' gun--a
deeper shot. Vance's rifle had a higher "pop". It was
hard to tell, but I think I recall that Jones' gun did
fire first. Didn't mention it during the argument because I didn't think it was any of my business. Vance
might be alive today if I had mentioned it.

FRANK JONES. Father of Charles Jones. His son would
never have killed anyone over a little hunting
incident, he didn't settle disputes that way.

CHARLES JONES. I live alone since I was divorced from
my wife and children three years ago. I didn't know
that Vance was tracking that bear. I saw the bear and
fired. Vance fired just a few seconds after me. He
was furious with me, but I told him since I fired
first, it was my bear. He was yelling and screaming so
much I figured let him have it if he was going to be
that way about it. After that our hunting party sort
of broke up and each went his own way. I had a few
drinks at Chuck's Place and went directly home, watched
a little television, and went to bed around 10:00 pm.
The next thing I knew was Sheriff Clayton banging on my
door. I surrendered without giving any trouble.
Clayton wanted to know where my Bowie knife was. I
told him he could find it in my jeep parked out front.
I guess someone must have taken the knife from my jeep.

The Prosecution and Defense attorneys agreed to stipulate that there was a poker game in Chuck's back room
on Friday night. Efforts to locate and identify
players were fruitless because no one would jeopardize
themselves by admitting to gambling illegally.

THE LINDSAY CASE

Is Dr. Lindsay guilty of the first degree murder of Mr. Butler?

In 1873, Benjamin Rush Butler, a prominent St. Louis railroader and social leader, died of unexplained causes [due to the state of the art of autopsy at that time]. Owing to the diligence of Sgt. Biggs of the St. Louis Police Department, the following intriguing facts became known and Dr. Lindsay was charged with the first degree murder of B. R. Butler.

ANN LOUIS BUTLER. Now married to Dr. Lindsay, was at the time of her father's demise, engaged to Dr. Lindsay. Miss Butler admitted to the inheritance of $450,000., the largest amount ever probated in St. Louis up to that time. Miss Butler could not understand why her father did not approve of Dr. Lindsay, but her father desired that she not marry Lindsay. Her father did finally agree to give her away at her wedding, but he died shortly before the wedding took place. Cross-Examination: Denied that her father was extremely unhappy with her proposed marriage to Lindsay; denied that she and her father quarreled; denied that her father would disinherit her if she married Lindsay.

GEORGE RAMUS. Has been butler in the Butler home for the last sixteen years. Toward the end of Mr. Butler's life, he took to quarreling with Miss Butler. I never heard exactly what was said because of the thick walls and oak doors of the mansion, but I know quarreling when I hear it.

MILES HARDWICK. The owner of a stockbrokerage firm in St. Louis, he testified that just before his death, Mr. Butler was engineering the largest "railroad deal" around St. Louis. Butler had secretly bought right-of-way to land along the Mississippi River and into downtown St. Louis so that the competing railroad, the St. Louis and Midland Railroad, would be unable to compete and hence go into bankruptcy; whereupon Butler would buy the St. L. & M. R. R. to merge it with his own and then sell his monopoly to the Central Illinois Railroad for a projected overall profit of $250,000. to Mr. Butler. His untimely death caused these plans to die in his mind, if you will excuse the expression.

STANHOPE BARTON. Has been Mr. Butler's solicitor for the past 35 years. Mr. Butler was absolutely infuriated that Miss Butler was to marry that Dr. Lindsay, whom Butler considered "effete and effeminate" and "a scoundrel out to get his [Butler's] money and daughter, to boot!" Butler had told him to prepare a new will to leave his daughter $5,000. and the rest of his estate to charity. Unfortunately, Butler died before he could sign the new will. In his opinion, Barton was sure that Butler let it slip to his daughter about the change in the will because Butler would frequently lose his temper and divulge business matters not in his best interest to do so.

DR. CADWALLANDER COLDEN. Had been Mr. Butler's personal physician for the last ten years. Mr. Butler was a hard worker, and often overworked. Toward his last days, I was prescribing digitalis for urinary disorders from which Mr. Butler suffered. I last saw Butler three days before his death. I gave him enough digitalis to last five days, and told him not to listen to any diagnosis Lindsay had to offer. Frankly, I was a bit put out with Lindsay's contradictions of my medications from time to time.

SGT. BIGGS. Investigated Butler's room, and found about 2 1/2 days of digitalis left in his bottle which he kept in his room. The room was well-kept, and there was no disorder. The bottle was identified by Cadwallander to be the bottle of digitalis which he gave to Butler. Biggs found Butler slumped over in his bedside chair with a half-empty bottle of bourbon left and the obvious smell of bourbon around Butler's body. Biggs never saw the bottle again. Cross-Examination: Dr. Lindsay and Miss Butler were descending the staircase as he was ascending. When he got back to the room, the bottle was gone. Direct-Examination: He did not actually see Lindsay have the bottle, but then he was not looking for one at that time. It was entirely possible for Lindsay to have taken the bottle, which I think is exactly what he did.

CLARA HART. Maid, testified that she had summoned the police and Miss Butler who was at Dr. Lindsay's residence, by messenger. Coincidently, Miss Butler and Lindsay arrived a few minutes after Sgt. Biggs arrived. Lindsay looked especially agitated and rushed Miss Butler up to Mr. Butler's room. Sgt. Biggs came down to question the staff and to leave them alone with the deceased. Dr. Lindsay then rushed Miss Butler out of the house in order to go to Church to pray for the deceased.

DR. BOWEN. Amicus curiae. Testified that digitalis in mild doses acts as a diuretic and mild stimulus. In large doses, especially in men in Mr. Butler's physical condition, it would overstimulate the heart and cause death by heart failure. Digitalis can be dissolved in any liquid, it still maintains its properties, and is practically tasteless. Any medical doctor has access to digitalis.

JOHN KEEL. Doorman at the Butler home, testified that he admitted Dr. Lindsay and Miss Butler on Tuesday evening. They went straightaway to the second floor drawing room where Mr. Butler spent much of his spare time. I could faintly hear arguments. The door opened once because the noise became louder for a few minutes; the door opened again, evidently to let in the person who left the room. Dr. Lindsay and Miss Butler left a few minutes later, having only stayed about ten minutes. Mr. Butler was furious, told me he was not to be disturbed further that evening, and went to his bedroom. That is the last time I ever saw him alive, as Sgt. Biggs and Miss Butler and Dr. Lindsay were called back when Mr. Butler's body was found. Cross-Examination: He never actually saw anyone leave or go back, because he was standing on the landing. Steadfastly maintained that the door (because of the sound difference) did open and close twice.

DR. LINDSAY. Did not murder Mr. Butler. Had often tried to mediate between Butler and his fiancee, but Butler always became furious and they had to leave. He did not leave the room on Tuesday night. He opened the door twice with the expectation to go, and then finally did go. Admitted that he was 37 years old and that Miss Butler was 24 years old. His practice kept him comfortable, but he was not a wealthy man by any means. He married Miss Butler two days after her father's death to help to console her. He never saw any bottle in Mr. Butler's room, never smelled any bourbon, and rushed Miss Butler to church because she needed spiritual revival at that particular time. In his opinion, Mr. Butler died from natural causes, and Sgt. Biggs has concocted the whole story to get a much needed promotion at the Police Department. Denied ever using digitalis because he felt it was "unsafe" for general use. Denied knowing about or discussing with Miss Butler the fact that she was to be cut out of the

70

will. He would have married her anyway because he
loved her.

THE STEELE CASE

Is Kirk Steele guilty of the first degree murder of von Otto?

This strange and grisly case arose in 1884 in the cave regions of southern Indiana. The community was somewhat divided over the issue of the prosecution's bringing the case to court, but people did have to admit that the case was not as open and shut as it first appeared. The prosecution tried the case under the following law: "Whosoever shall take the life of another human being, intentionally and not spontaneously, shall be guilty of first degree murder." The prosecution tried Kirk Steele for the murder of von Otto.

HARRY BEAMIS. The party of four was in my inn on Saturday night, they had dinner, and then retired to their rooms. The next day, they ate a hearty breakfast, as they told me they were to explore the caves in our region. When they mentioned that they would try Finegal's Cave, I told them that the cave was considered dangerous by the local people, and that no one ever went in it. They all appeared friendly as they left my inn to go exploring.

DORIS HARDY. As waitress at the Beamis Inn, she overheard the four men at breakfast say they would explore Finegal's Cave. She is pretty sure she remembers Mr. Steele telling Mr. Murray that is was silly to go in that cave after what they heard from Beamis. In all other respects she agrees with Mr. Beamis' statements. On cross-examination, she was asked how she knew the men's names. She answered that Steele was a friendly man, and that he had stayed around the table on the night before just talking. Business was slow that night and she was glad to have someone to talk to. When pressed on the names of the other men, she admitted that she could not remember them, but did maintain that Steele did say that to one of the men.

JOHN BINGLE. Had lead the rescue party after Beamis told the local constable that a party of men who had supposedly explored Finegal's Cave had not returned. We first explored the other caves in the immediate area (we were afraid to explore Finegal's Cave because it is known to the local people as a dangerous cave; if only those men from Ohio would have listened to Mr. Beamis' good advice). It took us two days to determine that they were not in any of the usual caves, and since they had not returned, we resolved to enter Finegal's Cave. Only two men, including myself, would even enter the cave. We proceeded approximately two miles into the cave when we met a blocked passage. It took us seven days to finally reach the four men, and only one of them was alive.

GEORGE BINGLE. Brother of John, testified that the three men took most of the third day just digging out very small rocks, dirt, and pebbles from the passageway--that is the reason the cave is so dangerous--the small rocks can cave-in much easier than large boulders, and although they are easier to move, they pack much tighter, thus slowing down rescue efforts. When we had finally cleared the passage, we were horrified to find the legs of a man, later identified as Murray, sticking out of yet another cave-in.

ARTHUR STOCK and JOHN REED both testified that they had joined the rescue party after the third man could no longer take it. They joined the Bingle brothers because at least they were convinced the men were in the cave and maybe someone could be found alive. The four of them worked for two days to clear the second cave-in, and remove Murray's body. The deep interior of the cave had split in a fork, and they unfortunately took the wrong fork, and went to the end of it and never found anyone. They backtracked, and proceeded approximately a mile into the other fork, and there they found Steele alive, the other men were dead.

DR. RAYMOND testified that the two bodies found in the vicinity of Steele were in such a state of advanced decomposition, owing to the humidity of the cave, that he could not determine the cause of death.

CONSTABLE THACKERY testified that he investigated the scene when he was notified of the find. There was no food, that is of the kind normal human beings eat, found. It was obvious that Steele had eaten from both of the dead bodies because flesh was missing from the thighs and upper arms of both bodies. It was a grisly sight. He had not gone on the search party because he had important business in the community to attend to. Thackery admitted that Steele was on the point of death, was delirious when they found him, and that it was a miracle that he even survived.

BENNY STOAKE. Was the third man in the original party, he could not stand the pressure in the cave of looking for those men, and he had to quit. He testified that the Bingle brothers and he often called out to see if anyone was alive. Stoake knew they were wasting their breath. The rocks were so tightly packed that no voice would have gotten through. Although he could not testify about the second passage blockage directly, he is sure that the same situation would have occurred there, too.

KIRK STEELE. Testified the party of four explorers went from Ohio to Indiana to do an interesting cave. That they were warned not to go to Finegal's Cave, that he was not in favor of it, but went along with the others. Murray was lost in the first cave-in, and there was no way they could have saved him at all. The three men were running away from the cave-in when another one occurred, but they just kept running as best they could to get away from it. Their lights were practically exhausted, so they conserved them. Their meager food-supply run out after two days, they really had only enough for a lunch because they were to return to the Inn for dinner. They had enough water from a small cave spring which ran through their part of the cave. The three of us made a pact to kill one person at a time in order that someone would hopefully survive. On what he thinks was the fourth day, Smith committed suicide by slashing his wrists rather than being killed by Steele and von Otto. Steele and von Otto subsisted on Smith for two days, or so he thinks, because both men were beginning to be very weak, and lose track of time. Sometime on the fifth or sixth day, he had to kill von Otto in order to survive. It is indelicate to say, but he must, that not all of the bodies were edible, and that all of them had trouble keeping the flesh down. He could not remember being rescued, he had made his peace. Maintained that the pact was agreed upon by all three men, that it was not murder in the traditional sense, that he was merely the "lucky" one by the luck of the draw, but now it looks as if he was the unlucky one for living.

STOCK and REED, recalled, testified that they did not observe any murder weapon such as a gun. They did find a knife with a small amount of blood dried on the edge of the blade. There were several medium size rocks which were loose in the area which could have been used to kill von Otto. There was no blood on any of the rocks.

Several character witnesses journeyed from Ohio to testify to Steele's good moral and Christian character. He was married, and was the father of three children, ages 7, 11, and 13. The prosecution was unable in cross-examination to prove that any dislike, hatred, or animosity was known to exist between any of the four men. The prosecution did ask if any of these witnesses could testify to what went on in Steele's mind in the cave. The defense objected, and the question was stricken from the record.

THE WARNER CASE

Is Denise Warner guilty of the first degree murder of William Warner?

DORIS BLACK, next door neighbor of the Warner's, heard a gunshot, or maybe more than one shot--she could not be certain--and called the police. She did not notice any unusual activity at the Warner residence, nor did she see anyone come or go.

DETECTIVE ROBERTS answered the police call, and made the following report. He found a dead white male, age 48-52, seated at a desk chair, slumped over a desk in the den of the home. He located one bullet hole approximately two inches above the right ear. (Ballistic experts later reported that the most likely posture, given the entrance route of the bullet, was that the deceased was seated at his desk.) French doors, which opened to an outside garden patio, were open. There were no visible signs of forced entry. There were no fingerprints on the outside of the doors. The deceased fingerprints, although partly smudged, were found on one door knob on the inside. Roberts noticed a .38 calibre handgun on the floor. It was one foot from the desk; the gun had been fired recently; three bullets were missing; the deceased's fingerprints were on the gun.

DENISE WARNER testified that she had not lived with her husband for the last eighteen months. She knew things were not well between her and her husband, but that she was shocked when he had his lawyer serve her with the divorce papers. She said that she was unable to have their two college-age children live with her because her husband gave her barely enough to survive on each month. He was a very selfish man, and over the years of their married lives, he had spent large sums of money on his silly glass collection, often to the deprivation of family life. On the afternoon of the death of her husband, she had two appointments to show real estate, which job she felt was fortunate to have in her economic condition. She showed the Johnson residence at 1:30--2:45 in the afternoon (corroborated by Johnson's in a deposition) and returned to the office to pick up the Morris family to show the Johnson residence (also corroborated by the Johnson's), at around 3:15 pm. She did not shoot her husband.

LOUIS WOODELL, insurance investigator, was called to the house the next day. Glass panes in a locked display case, still locked, were smashed. He determined that six pieces of Tiffany glassware, and 9 objects of glassware in Art Deco style, were missing. The insured value of these fifteen pieces was $120,000. The entire collection consisted of 32 pieces valued at $185,000. Mrs. Warner had notified the insurance company of the loss of the glassware pieces. Immediately after the police had called Mrs. Warner to the residence, the house was "sealed" so that the pieces were actually missing when the police arrived.

JOHN SMITH, owner of Smith's Insurance Agency, testified that Warner had been a most successful insurance broker. He had a winning way with customers, and had been able over the years to build up a profitable and sizable clientele. Warner was actually 51 years old, had been married to Mrs. Warner for 27 years, they had two children in college, and Warner had not lived with his wife for the last two and one-half years. Warner said that his wife had been unbearable to live with in the past five years, and he finally forced her to leave the house.

The defense agreed to stipulate that the gun belonged to Mr. Warner. The prosecution granted that it could not explain why two bullets had been fired, nor were these two bullets or bullet holes found in the Warner house. The defense granted that the murder bullet was indeed fired from the murder weapon.

GEORGE SEABURY, friend and fellow glass collector, stated that Warner had only one interest, and that was his hobby of glassware collecting. Warner and he often went to the antique shows in the greater Philadelphia area. Warner was an avid collector. He had a reputation among the "regulars" at the shows for making some very astute purchases, and he was known to have a reputation for having one of the finest glassware collections of its kind in the greater Philadelphia area. Warner was a secretive man, and most people were not invited to see his collection. He, Seabury, counted himself lucky that Warner like him enough to show him his collection from time to time.

MANFREID GOTTENBURG was an expert in glassware. He testified that the pieces said to be in the Warner collection were quite desirable, and highly marketable. Glassware of that nature was not marked (because it would ruin its value), and could easily be sold on the market. Many collectors would be happy to own Warner's pieces, and would purchase them "with no questions asked." That is, in his expert opinion, why none of the glassware pieces have appeared in any of the usual shows and auctions. He doubted if they ever would.

MAXWELL CARRINGTON, of the law firm Carrington and Carrington, testified that Warner had told him to prepare divorce papers for his wife, Denise. Warner's suit alleged mental cruelty and incompatibility. Warner had already changed his will, which now excluded his wife, and left the money in trust for the children until they were 25 years old. For some inexplicable reason, Warner had not made any specific provisions for his glassware collection in his old will nor in the new one. As things legally stood, Mrs. Warner would collect the $120,000 insurance money. The divorce papers had been served to Mrs. Warner three days before his death. He did not know if Mr. Warner ever saw Mrs. Warner, because he was of the idea the two were estranged.

OFFICER DANIEL FLORY, of the Police Department, testified that he timed the car routes claimed by Mrs. Warner on the day in question. From the Johnson residence to the real estate agency and then back to the Johnson residence took on the average (he made three trips) 21 minutes, at the legal speed limit. When he exceeded the legal speed limit, he was able to do the round trip in 17 minutes. From the route Mrs. Warner claimed to have taken, to the Warner house, takes about 7 minutes each, or 14 minutes extra to the round trip. In his professional opinion, Mrs. Warner obviously had time to make a side-trip to the Warner house, kill Warner, and then proceed to the real estate agency to pick up the Morris's to return to the Johnson house to show it again. He wished he caught her speeding because he could have prevented a murder.

DENISE WARNER, re-direct, testified that she had been caught in traffic and could not have possibly made that preposterous trip the police accuse her of making. It is foolish to thing she could murder her husband and then cooly show a house without giving any visible signs of nervousness, fear, etc.

MR. and MRS. JOHNSON both testified that they could not determine any change in the demeanor of Mrs. Warner on the first or second showing. They saw her off and on

78

during both showings in order to answer questions, etc.

MR. and MRS. MORRIS testified that they saw nothing unusual about Mrs. Warner. Although they did not know her very well, they certainly found it hard to believe that Mrs. Warner could have a few minutes earlier just murdered her husband. Mrs. Warner was a good real estate sales person.

THE WARREN CASE

Is Pvt. Warren guilty of the first degree murder of Capt. Charles?

As Captain Charles led a charge toward a well entrenched Confederate position in the Battle of the Wilderness, he fell mortally wounded. Under withering fire, and because Capt. Charles was hit about two hundred yards from the Confederate position, Lieutenant Jones took command. Jones ordered a soldier to secure Charles' body and then ordered a retreat to the Union position from whence the charge ensued. Upon close examination of Charles, it was ascertained that he was not shot by the Confederate, but was shot in the back by one of his own men. An investigation ensued, and Pvt. Warren was charged with the first degree murder of Capt. Charles.

MAJOR HARPER, United States Army Medical Corps. I ascertained that Charles was shot in the lower right side of his back with massive damage to his kidney and that vicinity. There were no other wounds which could have caused death, except a few scratches which were caused as he was dragged back to position. I extracted the bullet and it was fired from a Colt .45 which is standard issue for the United States Army.

PVT. HARRISON. The Confederates were putting up a terrific barrage of rifle fire with occasional cannon fire. I heard Lieut. Jones order me to secure Capt. Charles' person and then to retreat to our old position. I secured Capt. Charles who was breathing very weakly. I had to drag him about fifty feet to safety. Somewhere in that time, Capt. Charles expired. Charles muttered a few indistinguishable words.

MAJOR HOOPER. Capt. Charles was a brave and courageous soldier. When Col. Johnson determined that a charge should be mounted against the Confederate entrenchment, I suggested that Capt. Charles' company should lead the charge. Charles could be counted on under fire and duress which we knew he would encounter. The coward who shot Capt. Charles should be hanged for his dastardly deed.

COL. JOHNSON. After Capt. Charles' charge failed, three subsequent charges were ordered by me. All three charges failed in their object. Fifty men were lost in the three charges. We occupied the Confederate position only when their line was pulled back two miles toward the East. I am recommending a Citation for Bravery to be awarded posthumously.

LIEUTENANT JONES. Captain Charles was a fine officer and a leader of men. He had a reputation among the men as a stern disciplinarian who brooked no nonsense or horseplay; consequently his company was in the highest esteem with his superior officers. Captain Charles was often given difficult assignments which he executed with bravado and success. He intimated to me a week before his death how he was certain he was to be promoted to Major in the next month or two at the most. Charles led the charge up and out of the trench. I followed about five feet behind him. The rest of the company was about two or three feet behind me, spread out across our line as they charged. The fire from the Confederate position was intense, but not too accurate from that range. Suddenly, Charles fell. As I had noticed two or three others who had fallen, I ordered the men to hit the ground. Harrison was near Charles, so I told him to secure Charles. I ordered a regrouping and then a retreat to our safe position. Our men had begun to open fire a little, but some men never fired at all as they were running hard and were unable to fire.

PVT. BRINKMAN. Warren was about eight feet to my immediate right as we charged. Charles was about ten feet in front of us. Warren charged out of the trench shooting his pistol. Some of the other men in the line were shooting their pistols as they had no rifles. Warren had no rifle. Pistol fire was doing little damage to the Confederate position because of the distance. I saw Capt. Charles fall, and it scared all of us. I heard the regrouping bugle and I was glad to hear it, and then the retreat bugle. That charge was suicidal as we lost five men to the Rebels in about one minute of charging.

PVT. CONNORS. While we were marching to the front, Pvt. Warren somehow lost or displaced his rifle. When Capt. Charles found out, he was furious. He ordered that Warren was to forfeit three meals while on the stiff march for losing his rifle. Warren cursed Charles under his breath, as any man would under the circumstances.

81

LIEUTENANT TEMPLETON. Capt. Charles often complained to me about the new recruits he was given. He considered them below the average abilities of soldiers he regularly knew. Warren was a conscript, and Charles had to watch men like Warren because they did not want to be in the Army and they did not understand or appreciate the utility of Charles' stern discipline. Charles often mused that the conscripts were worse than the Rebs, and that he would rather have the enemy in front of him than a conscript coward in back of him.

PVT. HOWARD. The night before the charge, Captain Charles ordered the men to assemble. He gave us a speech about how we were to be entrusted with charging the Confederate position. Any man who did not charge or follow orders would be Court-Martialed, Charles would personally see to that. We knew from the tone of his voice and rumors around camp that the charge was going to be murder for most of us. We would not stand a chance against the Confederate position. Two of my best friends went down beside me. I thanked God when we retreated.

PVT. ROSS. Capt. Charles was a stern leader but an effective one. I had been with Charles through three campaigns. Warren was a slacker and grumbled about Army discipline. Warren was incensed about losing three meals, and I heard rumors that he was out to get Charles. I warned Capt. Charles, who said that yellow coward Warren did not have the guts to do anything, but for me to keep an eye on Warren at any rate. Warren was close into Charles as they charged and Warren was the only one in that area who was using his pistol because the fool supposedly "lost" his gun.

PVT. THOMAS. I was a good friend of Warren's. He disliked the Army and all it stood for. He considered himself cannon fodder of Mr. Lincoln. Charles was particularly odious to Warren as the total embodiment of the whole military apparatus. Cross examination: Warren was furious over his losing three meals on that terrible march. I heard him vow to himself that as he lived, he would repay Charles for his gross overreaction to the rifle incident. Re-direct: I never heard him say he would kill Charles or anything of that nature. A lot of men, including Warren and myself, disliked Charles but not enough to murder him.

LIEUT. TEMPLETON (recalled). I heard rumors around the camp that Warren was out to get Capt. Charles. I never

82

paid any attention to them because Warren was such a coward. Only a coward like Warren would shoot a brave and courageous officer like Charles in the back.

TESTIMONY FOR PRACTICE IN DIRECT AND CROSS-EXAMINATION

GAYLORD SASH. I have known my good buddy Tom Watkins for three years and I go to high school with him. I have a `55 Chevy which I often take out at lunch time and cruise around with my girlfriend, Sue Ann. Tom has his father's `53 Buick, and let me tell you that it is sick, because we dragged once and I won by a least five car lengths. We were not drag racing on the day in question, and my girlfriend will verify that. Yes, I do have two speeding tickets: one for going 28 mph in a 25 mph zone, and another one for drag racing. I did have my car out the day Tom was arrested for speeding. Frankly, I was surprised because I and the other kids at school consider Tom a safe and cautious drive, frankly, sort of "square." The local police department likes to hassle teenagers like us for no reason at all other than to scare us and make themselves look good with the citizens because they have nothing better to do. Tom's arrest is another one of those trumped-up charges to make examples out of unlucky teenage drivers such as Tom and me.

JOHN WHITE. Aged 62, White has operated White's Fine Clothes in downtown Middlebury from 1939 to the present when his store was burned to the ground, along with severe damage to several other stores adjacent to his on Main Street. He admitted that business had declined in the past several years due to the new shopping mall, but that his leadership in the Downtown Merchant's Association would soon revitalize the whole downtown area once again. He acknowledged that he had increased his fire insurance protection two years ago because of inflation and that his insurance adjusters had informed him then that his $900,000. policy would have to be adjusted again in five years to keep abreast with inflation. He denied that he had unsuccessfully attempted to sell his complete store and wares for $700,000. to an upstate business consortium. White was in New York City at a clothiers' convention on the Saturday night his store burned, and three other clothiers at the convention corroborated this.

JOHN RAMEY. He was in Irene's back room playing cards. There were two tables of card players. Before the actual shooting, he was faintly aware of arguing at the other table. Could not actually hear what the deceased and defendant were arguing about, but contended that it was quite noisy. He looked over toward the other table

84

just as the defendant shot the deceased. Ramey testified that he would have done the same thing in similar circumstances. If anybody reached into their pocket, as the deceased did, well, Ramey would let them have it. He maintained that he did not come forward with his testimony until two months later because he was afraid of recriminations. He remembers the scene just as if it were yesterday, the scene was so awful. Denied drinking while at the card party. Admitted to being arrested once on loitering and twice for gambling, but he has always been released for lack of evidence.

HARRY KEEL. My brother and I were together on the night of November 7, the night my brother is alleged to have killed the deceased. My brother came over to our house at about 7:00 pm and he stayed until the TV movie was over at 10:30 pm. Admitted that his wife was at her weekly church circle meeting and that she did not return until about 10:40 by which time his brother had already left. He owns the local hardware store, is active in local civic organizations (has held office in one) and is deacon in the church. Admits that his brother did not get on well with the deceased, and that neighbors of the deceased heard the fatal gunshot sounds at precisely 10:20 pm. He reiterated that his brother did not leave his house until after 10:30 pm. Although he is very close to his brother, he stated: "I would not perjure myself nor lie for him."

DAVE BROOKS. Testified that he was at a weekly poker party at a friend's house where Okey Sands was also playing cards. Stated that although he was drinking, all of the other card players were also drinking as much as he was, and some even more. In the interval of card playing, he had lost $270., mainly to Sands. That he hit Sands with his fist when he caught Sands cheating. The other players told him to leave the game and house if he was going to act like that. He then went to Harry's Bar where he had a few more drinks and left about 11:30 pm (corroborated by Harry, the bartender). He admitted that police found the murder knife in his garage under some rags. He maintained that he had never seen the knife before, and that his finger prints were not found on the knife, and that some unidentified prints were found on the knife. He admitted that he could not really afford to loose the $270., but that he did not murder Sands.

ALONZO BOLOGNESE. Had been with the DeLuxe Fur Company

in the capacity of night watchman, when on December 9,
on his rounds in the store, he noticed three suspicious
men driving slowly in front of the store.   It was a
late model blue sedan.   When the sedan disappeared
around the corner, he continued his rounds, thinking
that nothing significant was going to happen after all.
About fifteen minutes later, almost on impulse, he
opened the door to the storage vault area.   He did not
know who was more surprised, I or those men.   The three
men evidently became frightened because they pushed
Bolognese over as they ran out of the store.   Later, he
was taken down to the police station to identify the
men who pulled the DeLuxe job.   Although the light was
dim, he would never forget those faces as long as he
lived.   Two of the faces had acne pock marks.   He
received a $300. bonus from the DeLuxe Fur Company.

About the Author

Halford Ryan graduated from Wabash College in 1966, and received the M.A. in 1968 and the Ph.D. in 1972 from the University of Illinois. He is professor of public speaking and Director of Forensics at Washington and Lee University, Lexington, Virginia. He has coached student debaters in National Debate Tournament and audience-style debate formats. For the latter style, his debaters have argued before local, regional, and national collegiate audiences, as well as abroad before the English and Scottish debating unions. He has developed this book from his teaching of argumentation and debate for pre-professional and pre-law students.

He edited and contributed to AMERICAN RHETORIC FROM ROOSEVELT TO REAGAN: A COLLECTION OF SPEECHES AND CRITICAL ESSAYS, and is co-editor of AMERICAN ORATORS BEFORE 1900: CRITICAL STUDIES AND SOURCES, and AMERICAN ORATORS OF THE TWENTIETH CENTURY: CRITICAL STUDIES AND SOURCES.

DATE DUE